DOCTOR
on a DIET

White Chocolate Celebration

CAKE. FOR 12" / 30cm CAKE:

- 600g / 1lb 5oz plain flour
- 10g / 2 tsp bread soda
- pinch salt
- 225g / 8oz white chocolate
- 250ml / 8 fl oz cream
- 225g / 8oz butter
- 400g / 14oz caster sugar
- 6 eggs
- 2 tsp lemon essence
- grated zest 1 lemon
- 335 ml / 11 fl oz buttermilk.

Beat sugar / butter. Beat in eggs to sug... cream. Melt choc + ... butter mix. Add melted coo... chocolate. Fold in flour / soda. ... buttermilk. Bake 180C x 1 hr... zest 10 min. Remove + cool.

DOCTOR
on a DIET

Dr Paula Gilvarry

GILL BOOKS

Gill Books
Hume Avenue
Park West
Dublin 12
www.gillbooks.ie

Gill Books is an imprint of M.H. Gill and Co.

© Paula Gilvarry 2018

978 07171 8313 5

In collaboration with Kristin Jensen
Designed by Fiachra McCarthy
Photography by Rob Kiveat of a Fox in the Kitchen
Styling by Charlotte O'Connell
Indexed by Eileen O'Neill
Printed by Liberdúplex, Spain

This book is typeset in Miller Text.
5 4 3 2 1

ACKNOWLEDGEMENTS

This book was a long time in gestation but was delivered in a rapid nine weeks. There are many to thank.

First, Tom Sigafoos for kickstarting the process with his expert publishing experience and advice. To Maria McLoughlin for her deadly accurate cooking assistance and equally deadly humour during those nine weeks. To my good friend Claire Ronan, my diet buddy and style adviser. To Anne Loughlin, who kept me motivated weekly over this past year.

My recipes are inspired by good produce. I thank Mary McDonnell in Tír na nÓg, Charlie the Fish, every Friday in Sligo's Market Yard, Bismillah Asian supermarket for herbs, spices and exotic ingredients, and Jahanara and Ahmed for their superb lessons in Indian cooking. To Cecilia, for her many lessons in Jollof rice, and Naomi McBride for her many inspirational ideas.

Growing and cooking my own produce is a constant joy. For this I thank Hans Wieland and the team at the Organic Centre, Rossinver, for their many weekend classes. Also, Billy Kelly and Ronnie Gordan who have become my expert polytunnel advisers and waterers when I'm away.

To Sarah Speares, for her steady friendship and culinary assistance over 30 years.

My GP, Damian Tiernan, and my consultant cardiologist, Blaithnead Murtagh, for helping me stay well.

To Niall Molloy for his excellent critical eye and acerbic wit.

To my husband, Damien Brennan, who has been my constant companion and champion of my varied interests. To my wonderful children, Sarah and Paul, who have become outstanding adults and excellent creative cooks.

To my amazing food stylist, Charlotte O'Connell, and food photographer, Rob Kiveat, for making it look every bit as good as it tastes. Thanks, finally, to Deirdre Nolan and all the others at Gill Books who put such effort into making this all happen.

CONTENTS

INTRODUCTION

Medice, cura te ipsum
(Physician, heal thyself)

I have had a lifelong passion for food. Like most passionate relationships, though, food and I have had our ups and downs. As a public health doctor, wife and mother of two children – and as a woman who can gain weight just by walking near the dessert trolley – I've learned a few things about my relationship with food.

It's complicated.

Food has been my friend and my key to good health, but it has also led me into temptation and disaster. I've learned how to establish a loving relationship with food and I've created some delicious recipes along the way.

I grew up in the 1970s, in the post-Twiggy era when all the women in magazines were as lean as greyhounds. I have a curvy figure, but as an impressionable teenager I misread that and started dieting when I was 16. By now I've tried them all. High-fibre, low-fat, cabbage

soup – you name it, I've done it. I even tried a very low-calorie diet that puts your body into ketosis – in other words, starvation mode – which gave me constant bad breath and my skin and hair suffered. I lost two stone, but when I went back to my old eating habits, I gained back three.

Diets don't work. Certainly not for me.

During my career as a public health doctor and while raising my two children, I had a second profession. My husband, Damien, and I owned and operated Reveries Restaurant in Rosses Point, Co. Sligo, from 1985 to 1991. We designed Broc House overlooking Lough Gill, our home since 2002, and have a large, well-equipped kitchen and utility room so that we can host big gatherings of friends and family members plus the visitors who come to Sligo to learn about the landscape and culture that influenced William Butler Yeats through our Yeats Experience meals and tours.

I was also heavily involved with medical politics and was President of the Irish Medical Organisation (IMO) from 2006 to 2007. I spent a lot of time on the train to and from Dublin and had to attend many dinners and conferences. I had lost weight before I became President, but it soon piled on again, and then some. I also had high blood pressure and high cholesterol.

'As a Public Health Doctor, I had encountered overweight children and adults. I gave lifestyle advice to them and ignored my own weight issues.'

When I retired from public health medicine in 2014, I weighed nearly 17 stone. For my American friends, that's 238 pounds – and I'm only 5'2". I had arthritis in my knees and a dodgy back that caused sciatica (pain down my leg caused by a pinched nerve). I couldn't exercise by walking or cycling. I tried AquaFit, but it wasn't easy to make time for exercise.

I'd given up on dieting and ate whatever I wanted – sweets, chocolate, ice cream, crisps, bread – classic comfort eating. These sugary, salty, starchy treats were my reward after a long day of work and an evening of looking after the children, homework, cooking, cleaning and laundry. When I could sit down, I reached for the chocolate bar in my apron pocket. I liked a glass of red wine with meals, and of course one glass is never enough. (Did you know that there are 750 calories in every bottle?)

It's no joke to say that obesity comes with a lot of baggage. In 2016 I started to realise that if I didn't do something, I'd end up as a fat old lady who couldn't run after her grandchildren, destined to be bedridden in a nursing home. As a public health doctor, I had encountered overweight children and adults. I gave lifestyle advice to them but ignored my own weight issues, not to mention my high cholesterol, high blood pressure and arthritis.

By the summer of 2017 my weight issues were no longer simply a nuisance. Being obese had become a chronic problem while I spent my days cooking for a steady stream of Yeats Experience visitors. My hips hurt, my knees hurt and my back hurt.

In July I developed palpitations (a very fast heartbeat). I'd had palpitations in the past, but I'd been reassured that they weren't serious. As a doctor I would have advised any patient with palpitations to slow down, but like most doctors I ignored my own advice. I kept to my hectic schedule but I was very tired, slept poorly and had difficulty climbing stairs.

After three days of struggling I went to my GP, who did a heart tracing and confirmed that I had atrial fibrillation. Atrial fibrillation (AFib) is a fast, irregular heartbeat that

results from damage to the electrical system of the heart. The faulty electrical system triggers the heart to beat out of sync, damaging the heart muscle. Blood clots can form in the heart chambers, and if the fibrillation continues the clots can break loose and travel to the brain, causing a stroke.

'My challenge was to come up with tasty ideas for meals to stop myself from feeling deprived or getting bored. I started using lots of fresh herbs, spices and seasonings.'

My GP sent me straight to the Galway Clinic emergency department for assessment and admission. My poor husband was having a lie-in after a busy weekend of Yeats Experience visitors, but I had to wake him up to drive me to Galway. Cardiologist Dr Blathnaid Murtagh put me on medication and I spent four days hooked up to monitors until my heartbeat returned to normal.

I stayed on beta blockers and blood thinners as well as my other medications, but the AFib returned. My cardiologist put me on Dronedarone, a stronger medication, but also advised me that for every 10% of body weight I could lose, I would reduce the risk of reverting to AFib by 15%. At this stage I

had lost over a stone (14 pounds), but hearing this was the impetus I needed to keep going. I knew I would have to stay on the anti-arrhythmic meds, but I wanted to stay well.

I decided that I would try to continue to lose weight slowly. I had been following the Motivation weight loss programme, which is a combination of a diet plan and cognitive behavioural therapy. The programme uses a low-carbohydrate, low-fat and high-protein diet plan. My challenge was to come up with tasty ideas for meals to stop myself feeling deprived or getting bored. I started using lots of fresh herbs, spices and seasonings. I'm also lucky to have my own free-range eggs and a polytunnel full of organic salad ingredients.

Since my AFib diagnosis in the summer of 2017, I have lost five stone – that's 70 pounds. I no longer need blood pressure medication and since my cholesterol is normal I can drop the statin meds. I check my blood pressure regularly, get my cholesterol checked every six months and have regular GP and cardiology check-ups. I need to stay on Dronedarone to stabilise my heartbeat and Apixaban to prevent clots indefinitely, but because I have reduced my weight by 25%, I have reduced my risk of atrial fibrillation, and its scary consequences, by 40%.

I now weigh 11 stone 9 pounds (or 163 pounds) and I feel great. My challenge now is to keep the weight from creeping back on. I have learned how to understand and control my comfort eating impulses and how to get back on track after a slip. I keep a food diary. I plan my meals and treats in advance and I amend those plans if circumstances change during the day. When I eat out, I choose the healthiest options. If I decide to have pasta, potatoes or rice, I will have a small portion of that starchy food and a smaller dessert. I still like a glass of wine, but I have a two-glass limit now and I drink loads of water.

This year my angiogram showed that I have perfect, fully functioning coronary arteries. I'm walking, practising Pilates and starting to cycle. I'm busy looking after my hens, my two Labradoodles, my vegetable garden and my polytunnel. Damien and I are still hosting Yeats Experience visitors and I'm still cooking up a storm.

In the past year, I have succeeded in losing five stone (70 pounds) of fat, not muscle or fluid. I still need to lose a little more, but I have devised recipes for the kind of healthy food that I can cook and enjoy for the rest of my life. Those recipes are in this book. I'm happy to be able to share them with you.

Paula Gilvarry
March 2018

KEYS to HEALTHY LIVING

There are four main aspects of healthy living: nutrition, water, exercise and social life.

NUTRITION

It's an interesting word, nutrition. It doesn't encompass all the emotions that go with food. Food keeps us alive and well, but there is so much more to food than that. I love all aspects of food – reading about it, talking about it, cooking it, tasting it, eating it and sitting at the table with family or friends over a meal.

I'm not going to give you an in-depth essay on nutrition here, but rather will outline the basics to help you to make the right food choices while later on giving you tasty, healthy recipes to facilitate these choices. The main thing you need to know is that there are three main nutrients in food – carbohydrates, fat and protein – and you need them all in a balanced diet. Fibre, vitamins and minerals also play an important role and good gut health is getting an increasing amount of attention these days too.

CARBOHYDRATES

There are two types of carbohydrates: simple carbohydrates and complex carbohydrates.

Simple carbohydrates

Simple carbohydrates include sugars like fructose and sucrose. Fruit, milk and honey naturally contain simple sugars. The simple sugars in natural foods have the advantage of also containing vitamins, minerals and fibre. Fibre is harder for our stomach to digest, which slows down the rate at which sugar goes into our system.

Refined simple sugars are found in processed foods such as fizzy drinks, sweets, cakes and syrups. They go through your system very quickly and get into the bloodstream rapidly – think of children after a birthday party,

swinging off the curtains at bedtime. When you consume refined sugars like biscuits or fizzy drinks, your body gets a sudden surge of sugar and produces insulin to bring your blood sugar levels down again, so you quickly go from high to low. You get a short-lived burst of energy, followed by a slump that leaves you tired, cross and with a bad case of the munchies.

> *'Good fats help our blood circulation and immune system, but bad fats harm our health and can cause arteries to harden.'*

The key thing to remember is that sugar is sugar, whether it's a natural sugar or refined sugar. Many natural foods, such as dates and honey, are loaded with sugar, so eat them in small amounts.

Complex carbohydrates

Examples of complex carbohydrates are grains and pulses. Complex carbohydrates take longer to metabolise because they contain fibre, which means they release sugar and energy more slowly. They also contain important vitamins and minerals. These are the good starches that can help you lose weight or maintain a healthy weight.

In short, keep away from the sweets, fizzy drinks and the high fructose corn syrup they contain, but don't forget that natural carbohydrates like fruit and fruit juice still contain sugar too. Go for the complex carbs such as green vegetables, wholegrains, sweet potatoes, beans, lentils and peas.

FAT

Not all fat is bad. Fats, or lipids, are essential for the proper functioning of our cells, especially those of our nerves and our brain. Omega-3 and omega-6 fatty acids help our body take in vitamins like A, D, E and K, which need fat in order to be absorbed into the bloodstream. Good fats help our blood circulation and immune system, but bad fats harm our health and can cause arteries to harden, leading to heart attacks and strokes.

Fats are divided into unsaturated, saturated and trans fats. To make things even more complicated, unsaturated fats are further subdivided into monounsaturated and polyunsaturated.

Unsaturated fats

Monounsaturated fats are found in olive oil, nut oils, avocados, nuts and seeds. The Mediterranean diet is rich in these foods and thus reduces the amount of 'bad' cholesterol (LDLs) in our blood. LDL cholesterol can cause heart disease, clogged arteries and stroke.

Polyunsaturated fats are found in oily fish, walnuts, flaxseeds and vegetable oils. The main polys are omega-3 and omega-6. Our bodies can't make these, so we have to get them from our food. Try to have more omega-3s (found in oily fish, flaxseeds and walnuts) than omega-6s (found in soya beans, sunflower oil and rapeseed oil).

Saturated fats

These include butter, coconut oil, fatty beef, lamb, chicken skin and cheese. Saturated fats should be eaten in moderation, but you don't have to avoid them completely.

Processed low-fat foods replace the fat with sugar or sweeteners, salt and other ingredients to make them taste better. I eat cheese but I hate the processed low-fat kinds, so I have a smaller amount of the full-fat stuff. I sometimes go to the Cloona Health Retreat in Westport, Co. Mayo, and I remember asking Darragh, the owner, for advice on diet. He said, 'Up your standards! Eat the best chocolate, steak and cheese and drink the best wine you can afford, but eat less of them.'

Trans fats

Trans fats are used in processed foods to make them last longer and to make things like cereals crunchier. They are very bad for you. They increase your levels of 'bad' cholesterol, reduce your levels of 'good' cholesterol, make it easier to put on weight and may put you more at risk of heart disease, so limit the deep-fried takeaways and processed sweets, biscuits, pies and pastries.

PROTEIN

Our bodies need protein for muscle building and muscle repair, strong skin and nails, and to make antibodies, enzymes and hormones.

Proteins are slowly digested in our stomach and require more energy to metabolise. Protein also helps you stay full for longer. Adding a little protein to each meal means you digest your food more slowly and it keeps your blood sugar levels steady, which in turn can help you avoid the munchies.

Complete protein foods are eggs, meat, fish, dairy products, chia seeds, quinoa and buckwheat. Less complete protein foods are pulses, nuts, seeds, grains and vegetables.

THE ROLE OF FIBRE

I have suffered from constipation all my life, especially when I went on one of my mad diets. When I was a medical student in Galway in the 1970s, Professor Burkitt was advocating a high-fibre diet to help with diverticulitis (inflammation) in the bowel and to help prevent bowel cancer. We were shown photos of large stools from native Africans and of puny European attempts. I remember going home and telling my mum about what I had learned and she and my granny, both martyrs to constipation, started eating bran bread and loads of potatoes and were delighted with the results.

Some fibre-rich foods, like the inner parts of oats, bran, pulses, beans, fruit and vegetables, are soluble, which means that they take in water in the bowel and soften the stool. Others, like the outer husk of oats and

barley, nuts, seeds, popcorn, and the skins of fruit and vegetables, pass through the bowel undigested and bulk up the stool so that it moves along the bowel better.

Fibre also keeps us fuller for longer, helps regulate blood sugar levels and can reduce 'bad' LDL cholesterol.

VITAMINS

If I had a euro for every person who came to my GP surgery looking for vitamins, I would be a rich pensioner now. Yes, we need vitamins and minerals, but we get most of them from a properly balanced diet. Certain medical conditions can lead to vitamin deficiencies, but apart from vitamin D, the general population can get everything they need simply by eating a good, mixed diet.

> *'Apart from vitamin D, the general population can get everything they need simply by eating a good, mixed diet.'*

Vitamin A

Vitamin A is found in orange and yellow vegetables (we all know about carrots and eyesight!) as well as green vegetables, fish oils, milk and eggs. It plays a major role in eye health for the retina (back of the eye), the cornea and the covering of the eyeball. It's also important for repairing and making our cells, so it plays a key role in skin health (in a synthetic form, retinol, which is another term for vitamin A, has a role in skin conditions like psoriasis and acne), in our immune system and in maintaining the health of our heart, lungs and kidneys.

B vitamins

There are eight B vitamins. They all play an important part in metabolism, but vitamins B9 and B12 are particularly important.

Folic acid (vitamin B9) is essential for cell growth, especially in the first trimester of pregnancy, when the baby's brain and spine are developing. This is why all women who are planning a pregnancy or as soon as they know they are pregnant are advised to take folate supplements. Folic acid is found in green vegetables and grains.

Vitamin B12 (cobalamin) works with folic acid in important cell functions like making DNA, red blood cells and nerve components and is important for the immune system. Most vitamin B12 is found in animal sources, so vegans and vegetarians need to make sure they are getting an adequate amount of B12.

Vitamin C

Vitamin C is found in citrus fruits. It's important for making collagen for our skin. If you are deficient in vitamin C, you can suffer from bleeding gums and cuts will be slow to heal.

Vitamin D

Irish people know all about vitamin D – or rather, the lack of it. We go to the Continent in droves to get a blast of sunshine after a long, dark, dreary winter (and often spring as well). A serious lack of vitamin D, which is absorbed by the skin from sunlight, can lead to rickets, but we usually just suffer from a calcium deficiency, as we need vitamin D to metabolise calcium. Calcium-rich foods include dairy products, green leafy vegetables and tinned fish like salmon, tuna and sardines.

We should all take a vitamin D supplement from September to March to counteract those dark days with minimal sunshine, and try to get a blast of sun whenever and wherever we can. I have a south-west-facing deck on my house and I have my chair permanently set up for that precious 10 or 20 minutes when I can bask in the glorious sunshine. Just remember the sunscreen if you are outside for longer then 20 minutes.

Vitamin E

Vitamin E is an antioxidant. It prevents damage to the outer part of red blood cells from free radicals – no, not Che Guevara! Free radicals are substances that can damage cells and can lead to cell ageing and cancer. Vitamin E is found in vegetable oils, almonds, avocados and spinach. Skin creams often have vitamin E added, as it is easily absorbed through the skin.

GOOD GUT HEALTH

In recent years, research has given us new information on how our gut works. The gut is an incredible system containing 2kg of bacteria that keep our immune system balanced and affect our brain as well. What we eat has a significant effect on our health, as the gut needs the proper fuel to function.

> *'We should all take a vitamin D supplement from September to March to counteract those dark days with minimal sunshine, and try to get a blast of sun whenever and wherever we can.'*

The gastrointestinal system (GIT, or gut) runs from our mouth to our rectum. It's a remarkable organ that does more than just digest food. The gut contains 500 trillion microbes (the microbiome). The many different varieties need to be kept in a healthy balance by eating the correct food. When there is a healthy balance of microbes, the benefits are remarkable. They regulate the immune system, help to regulate body weight and convert indigestible food into hormones and chemicals that play a role in our mood (our gut can talk to our brain through the vagus nerve), appetite and general health.

Prebiotics and probiotics both encourage good gut health. Foods that encourage a good balance of microbes in our gut are the prebiotics (which feed existing microbes), such as onions, garlic, leeks, greens and asparagus;

starches like grains, seeds, legumes, barley and oats; as well as seaweed and flaxseeds. Foods that encourage the growth of new microbes (probiotics) include full-fat cheeses and fermented foods like yogurt, kimchi, sauerkraut, kefir and raw apple cider vinegar. Milk kefir contains up to 50 types of live bacteria and yeasts. I make my own every day and you'll see that I use it in a lot of my recipes, including smoothies, overnight porridge, brown bread and as a marinade for fish and chicken. We have an apple orchard, so we also press our own apple juice and make our own cider and apple cider vinegar too.

WATER

Water is essential for good health. We need six to eight glasses of water a day (that's 2 litres or 4 pints), but you need more water if you're overweight. Space your water consumption throughout the day, ideally drinking about 250ml at a time. Buy a large reusable bottle and always keep it filled. Keep one in your bag, at your desk or in the car.

Water helps our muscles to function and keeps our skin healthy and clear. Our kidneys also need water to work properly. If they can't work well, the burden goes to our liver. The liver should be working at turning fat stores to energy, but if it has to do the kidneys' job too, it means less fat is processed, which in turn leads to weight gain.

Water is retained by the body if we don't drink enough. The body panics if it's not getting enough and holds onto every drop, which can make you feel bloated and give you swollen hands and ankles. The afternoon slump is related to dehydration as well – reach for a glass of water before you snack.

If you're having a glass of wine, always drink water as well. A good trick is to keep the wine on your left side and the water on your right (that is, by your dominant hand) so that you drink more water than wine.

As we get older we may be inclined to reduce our water intake. Elderly people need to be encouraged to drink enough water (too many trips to the loo, they will say), as dehydration can lead to confusion, falls and constipation.

EXERCISE

Now that I'm in my sixties, I realise just how important it is to be active. I don't mean extreme exercise – just getting off the sofa and moving around is good for you. I have seen too many older people lose their mobility, stuck in chairs and limited to a small area inside and around the house, to allow it to happen to me. Mobility means more than walking. It includes balance, dexterity and joint mobility (especially your shoulders, which are important for simple things like brushing your hair and putting on clothes).

The only way to stay healthy and mobile is to stay active. Move around as much as you can doing housework, a hobby, gardening, yoga or Pilates, a daily brisk walk, anything! The key, though, is to do something you enjoy. There's no point hating or dreading your exercise.

And don't wait until you're retired like me. Make exercise, hobbies and interests a good habit no matter what stage of life you're at so that when you do retire (or as I call it, refiring!) you have a good foundation to build on. Even small things like taking the stairs instead of the lift or taking regular breaks to stand up from your desk and walk around will make a big difference.

> *'Even small things like taking the stairs instead of the lift or taking regular breaks to stand up from your desk and walk around will make a big difference.'*

It takes more work to stay healthy as you get older, so go for regular check-ups, know your family health history, watch your weight, find exercise that you like and stay mentally active too by learning new skills, remaining curious and open to new experiences or even just doing crosswords or quizzes.

A HEALTHY SOCIAL LIFE

One of the top indicators for a long life is your social interactions. My 95-year-old mother-in-law has visitors every day who come not to cheer her up, but to be cheered up by her. She reads the papers, does the crossword, watches TV, goes shopping once a fortnight and meets loads of people as she shops.

We are social creatures and we all need other people. However, you don't need to become stressed by this or take it to extremes. Daily life is enough of a challenge on its own and navigating work and play isn't easy, especially if you're a full-time working parent. I worked a five-day week all through my children's school years and it was exhausting. You go from work to home, one job to another!

In between work commitments or your children's myriad after-school activities, it's important to make time for yourself too. Meet friends, go for a massage, do an exercise class, read a book – anything that gives you some down time to yourself, even if it's just for half an hour. Remember that you are a very important person and your family, friends and colleagues need you to stay well, so go for any check-ups you need, whether it's bloods, mammograms, smears, dexa scans or colonoscopies, and look after your eyes and teeth too. At work and in social situations (family too if you can manage it!), avoid the negative people, keep stress in check and always take your lunch and breaks away from the desk. Set an alarm on your phone to remind you to stretch or stand up and walk around every half hour.

Always keep some energy for your time at home with your partner or children. Be active with the children, whether it's a family walk, cycle or swimming lessons, as they will learn from you and the good example you set. Walk over the mess, spend time with your family and to hell with the housework!

TOP TIPS for WEIGHT LOSS

I still can't believe that I've managed to shed five stone (70 pounds) in a year. I look in the mirror and don't recognise this person smiling back at me. Buying clothes is a joy and I still marvel that I've gone from a size 22 to a size 14.

When you lose as much weight as I did, it's inevitable that people will ask you how you did it. There is no magic bullet or quick fix, but the answer is actually very simple: weight loss is all about taking in fewer calories than you use up. When following a healthy, balanced diet, men are allowed up to 2,500 calories per day and women get 2,000, but these numbers aren't set in stone for everyone and can vary due to your age, metabolism and level of activity, among other factors. Personally I don't have time for calorie counting and I know few people who do.

I've never thought of my weight loss as a diet, but rather a lifestyle and mindset change in the way that I cook, eat and think. If you follow these common sense tips and try the recipes in this book, you will lose weight and never feel deprived.

* Slow and steady wins the race when it comes to fat loss. There are plenty of diets out there that promise dramatic results in a short amount of time, but inevitably you just gain all the weight back – and then some – as soon as you come off the diet. Weight loss of approximately 1kg per week is a more realistic and sustainable goal.

* If you're worried about not being able to enjoy good food any more, don't be! Remember, you can still eat lovely food, just have less of it. Increase the quality of your ingredients and you won't mind reducing the quantity.

* Watch your portion sizes. A portion of protein should be the same size as your

fist for dinner or half the size of your fist for lunch and make up one-quarter of your plate. Carbs should make up another quarter and the rest of the plate should be vegetables or salad.

* Always reach for water before food. Chances are you're not that hungry, just dehydrated. Aim to drink 2 litres (4 pints) of water per day.

* Keep a food diary when you start your weight loss journey, as it will become immediately obvious what you need to cut out.

* Don't skip meals, as it wreaks havoc with your blood sugar levels. Never starve yourself either, as it will lead to losing muscle as well as fat. This is why people on extreme diets tend to look gaunt.

* As you get older you need to be careful not to lose muscle mass or you will end up looking haggard. Muscle also metabolises fat, so keep that muscle mass safe – again, no extreme diets!

* Keep a good supply of salad ingredients in your fridge for a quick, easy and healthy meal (see page 96 for more on this).

* The freezer is your friend! Keep extra dinner portions in individual containers in the freezer so that you can reheat them easily and in less time than it takes for a takeaway delivery to arrive.

* Use low-calorie cooking sprays in lieu of oils, as spraying rather than pouring oil will ensure you use much less and therefore will significantly reduce your calorie intake. If you don't like the idea of using a processed oil, buy a spray bottle and fill it with your preferred oil.

'Always reach for water before food. Chances are you're not that hungry, just dehydrated. Aim to drink 2 litres (4 pints) of water per day.'

* Cut out processed foods as much as possible. They contain lots of sugar, salt and fats and contribute to weight gain.

* It's so easy to grow your own fruit and vegetables. Start with a few herbs in a container in your back garden or on your kitchen windowsill – you'll be delighted at how much flavour fresh herbs or your own home-grown veg can add to food.

* If you must snack on the go, choose a protein bar, as they'll fill you up more. Check the nutritional information on the packet, though, as some have a lot of calories and some have so much sugar that you may as well be eating a chocolate bar.

* Avoid sugar as much as possible. You'll be surprised at how quickly your taste buds adjust and you'll soon find that you don't like very sweet things any more. Beware of hidden sugars, such as those in dried fruit and honey (see page 13 for more on this).

* Think about why you're reaching for food. Very often there is an emotional reason we're hungry rather than a physical one.

* Sit down to eat, set the table and eat slowly to truly enjoy your food.

* Ensure treats are just that – treats, not everyday foods.

* By all means enjoy a glass of wine, but limit your alcohol consumption when you're trying to lose weight, as it has a lot of empty calories and can promote unnecessary snacking too.

* Get active! To maintain a healthy weight you need at least 30 minutes a day of moderate activity (such as a brisk walk or cycling at 10mph) on five days a week (i.e. 150 minutes a week). When you're trying to lose weight, being physically active for 60–90 minutes every day will help you to achieve your weight loss goals. And of course don't forget that being active has a range of other benefits for your overall health and mobility.

* If you can't exercise at the moment, don't despair. When I was at my heaviest I couldn't walk very much, yet I still lost weight. The main thing is to stay off the couch and keep moving. I'm on my feet for up to 10 hours a day during the Yeats Experience high season.

* Once you've achieved your target weight, keep filling in a food diary. I know it's a pain, but it will become a habit and if you gain weight you can flick back through the diary to see where you may have overeaten or skipped meals.

* Don't go back to your old habits. Keep eating healthy food, keep treats as occasional indulgences and don't undo all your hard work by bingeing on junk food.

* You should have a smaller appetite after weight loss, so keep your portion sizes small.

* Throw out all the clothes that no longer fit you. I wear a belt, so I know what notch it should be at.

* Don't give up! If you fall off the wagon, just think of it this way: climbing back on will burn up some calories. Don't beat yourself up, just start again and look at your food diary to help you understand why you slipped. If there are any tempting treats left in the house, give them away. If I cook a dessert at the weekend, I always give away the uneaten half.

BREAKFAST

A year ago, before I started my weight loss journey, I rarely ate breakfast. I would then get hungry around 11 a.m. and would have toast, sausage rolls, cereal or rashers, then more toast and marmalade. By lunchtime I would go for a large cheese and ham sandwich and a slice or two of cake. I eventually realised that because I was eating so much high-sugar and high-carbohydrate food, I was asking my body to work too hard and was depriving my gut of a balanced mix of nutrients to keep it healthy and working for me.

So now I adhere to the old saying 'breakfast like a king, lunch like a prince, dine like a pauper'. I'll enjoy a baked avocado with eggs and tomato or a delicious courgette and mushroom frittata with a slice of my own brown bread. I eat within 20 minutes of waking up and I sit down at the table to take my time over the meal. I don't have to leave the house to go to work now that I'm retired, but if you can manage it, take a few minutes to sit down to eat and get your head together for the day ahead.

By dinnertime you'll realise that keeping your blood sugar levels steady throughout the day by having a good breakfast, lunch and snacks, you'll eat a smaller dinner and avoid any binges. So plan ahead and keep your fridge and cupboards stocked full of all the ingredients you need. Make up a batch of porridge or fruit compote, defrost some pancakes or make a quick frittata. Treat yourself to a royal breakfast every day.

PORRIDGE with APPLES, RAISINS and CINNAMON

When I was a child, we got our milk in a large milk can straight from the dairy. It was full-cream milk and my mum would pour it into wide-mouthed jugs until the cream settled on top. I got the job of skimming it into a bowl for whipping or putting on top of our porridge. Yum! These days I use my own homemade milk kefir instead of cream.

SERVES 2

100g jumbo porridge oats (not instant)

50g raisins

1 heaped tsp ground cinnamon, plus extra to serve

800ml cold water

2 Bramley apples, peeled and coarsely grated (about 350g grated weight)

4 heaped tbsp natural bio yogurt or milk kefir, to serve

1. Toss the oats, raisins and cinnamon in a large bowl. Pour in the cold water and stir to combine, then cover and leave to soak overnight on the countertop or in the fridge.

2. The next day, tip the contents of the bowl into a pan and stir in the grated apples. Cook over a medium heat, stirring frequently, for 5–10 minutes, until the oats are cooked and the apple is soft but still has a bit of bite and texture.

3. Reserve half of the porridge for the next day (see the tip) and spoon the remainder into two bowls. Top each portion with a spoonful of yogurt or milk kefir and dust with a pinch of cinnamon.

TIP:

You can buy milk kefir in supermarkets or health food shops. If you want to have a go at making your own, you can buy kefir grains online.

Porridge is easy to reheat the next day in bowls in the microwave or in a pan on the hob with an extra splash of milk or water.

Soaking the oats overnight makes them easier to digest.

BAKED AVOCADO with EGGS and TOMATO

This is a substantial breakfast or brunch served with a crispbread or a salad for a filling meal full of good oils and plenty of protein. It serves two as a hearty breakfast, but have just half an avocado if you're watching your calories.

SERVES 2

2 large ripe avocados,
halved and stoned

2 ripe tomatoes,
finely chopped

4 eggs

salt and freshly ground
black pepper

freshly grated Parmesan
cheese (optional), to serve

fresh basil leaves or snipped
fresh chives, to garnish

1. Preheat the oven to 180°C.

2. Scoop a little flesh out of each avocado half to make more room. Put the avocado halves on a baking tray. If they wobble too much, cut a little horizontal slice from the unpeeled side of each half so that they lie flat on the tray.

3. Divide the chopped tomatoes between the avocado halves, then carefully crack an egg on each avocado half. Season with salt and pepper.

4. Cook in the oven for 15–20 minutes, until the egg whites are set but the yolk is still soft.

5. To serve, scatter over a little Parmesan (if using) and garnish with torn fresh basil leaves or snipped chives.

ANYTIME EGGS

We reared hens at home and always had fresh eggs. Mum would preserve eggs in water in a large container in the autumn before the hens stopped laying and these eggs were then used for the dozens of Christmas cakes that she churned out every winter. Now that I keep my own hens I love knowing that I'm eating eggs from happy hens. Always spend the extra on free-range, organic eggs. It's worth it.

SERVES 1

olive oil cooking spray

2–3 cooked potatoes, sliced

a handful of cherry tomatoes, sliced

2 spring onions, sliced

salt and freshly ground black pepper

1 egg

a few fresh basil leaves, torn

1. Spray a frying pan set over a medium heat with the oil. Add the potato slices and fry on both sides until brown. Add the cherry tomatoes and spring onions and fry for about 1 minute, until softened. Season with salt and pepper, then make a well in the middle of the pan. Gently break the egg into the well and fry until it's cooked to your liking. I usually cook my egg for about 5 minutes, until the whites are set and the yolk is still a little runny.

2. Scatter over the basil leaves and serve.

OMELETTE WRAPS

I make a big batch of these to freeze or refrigerate for up to three days. Separate each wrap with a piece of non-stick baking paper before storing.

MAKES 2 WRAPS

2 eggs

20g Parmesan cheese, finely grated

freshly ground black pepper

olive oil cooking spray

1. Beat the eggs, Parmesan and a pinch of black pepper together in a small bowl.

2. Spray a non-stick frying pan set over a high heat with the oil. Pour half of the egg mixture into the pan, then immediately reduce the heat to low. Leave it alone for about 2 minutes to allow it to set before you try to flip it.

3. Ease the edges away from the sides of the pan with a spatula, then slide the spatula under the wrap and turn it over. Cook the other side for about 2 minutes more, until that side is set too.

4. Turn out onto a plate and cook the second wrap the same way.

5. You can eat these wraps hot or cold (see the storage information in the intro). Fill with chopped vegetables, salads, hummus (page 188) or anything that takes your fancy.

COURGETTE and MUSHROOM FRITTATA

This is my go-to recipe for a quick meal at any time. It's also a great vegetarian lunch option.
SERVES 4–6

olive oil cooking spray

1 medium courgette, halved lengthways and cut into 5mm-thick slices

170g chestnut or button mushrooms, thinly sliced

8 large eggs, beaten

salt and freshly ground black pepper

100g tinned butter beans, drained and rinsed (optional)

30g Parmesan cheese, grated

1. Preheat the oven to 180°C.

2. Heat 6–8 spritzes of oil in a large ovenproof non-stick frying pan over a medium heat. Add the courgette and mushrooms and cook for 4 minutes. Cover the pan with a lid and cook until the courgette is tender. Stir well, reduce the heat, cover and cook for 5 minutes, stirring occasionally. Remove the lid and cook, still stirring occasionally, until all the moisture in the pan has evaporated.

3. Meanwhile, crack the eggs into a large bowl, season with a little salt and pepper and whisk the eggs until well blended.

4. Add the butter beans to the pan (if using), then pour in the beaten eggs. Cook for 3 minutes, then remove the pan from the heat and scatter the grated Parmesan on top.

5. Transfer the pan to the oven. Bake for 10 minutes, until the eggs are set and cooked through – the tip of a knife inserted into the centre should come out clean.

6. Remove from the oven and leave to cool for 3 minutes. Loosen the edges with a spatula, then slide the frittata out of the pan onto a chopping board and cut into slices to serve.

> **TIP:**
>
> You could also use: leftover potatoes/pasta and cooked vegetables with chopped ham; crab and courgettes; rice and beans; kale and goats' cheese; smoked salmon and broccoli – frittatas are so versatile!

QUINOA PANCAKES

These gluten-free pancakes freeze beautifully, so make a big batch.

MAKES 6 PANCAKES

150g cooked quinoa
(see the tip)

2 large eggs, lightly beaten

1 tbsp cornflour

¼ tsp baking powder

¼ tsp ground cinnamon

¼ tsp vanilla extract

a pinch of salt

olive oil cooking spray

chopped fresh fruit, to serve

yogurt, to serve

1. Put all the ingredients except the oil, fruit and yogurt in a bowl and mix well with a fork.

2. Spray a large non-stick frying pan set over a medium heat with the oil. Use a serving spoon to add dollops of the quinoa mixture to the pan. Cook for 2 minutes, until you can see bubbles forming on the surface, then flip over with a spatula and cook for another 2 minutes.

3. Transfer to a warmed plate and continue with the remaining mixture, adding another spritz of oil to the pan if needed and stirring before pouring the mixture each time.

4. Serve the warm quinoa pancakes with chopped fresh fruit and yogurt.

TIP:

You can find packets of pre-cooked quinoa in most supermarkets now.

You can make a savoury version of these by leaving out the cinnamon and vanilla and adding 1 teaspoon of five-spice powder instead. The savoury pancakes can be served with chopped cooked chicken or hummus (page 188).

BANANA PANCAKES

These little pancakes are a lifesaver for breakfast on the run. Make them in batches and freeze them individually so that you can grab a few on your way out the door, as they thaw fairly quickly, or you can pop them in the microwave first.

MAKES 6 PANCAKES

40g oat bran

4 eggs

2 ripe bananas, mashed

½ tsp ground cinnamon

¼ tsp vanilla extract

butter-flavoured cooking spray

1. Put all the ingredients except the cooking spray in a food processor or blender and blitz to combine into a smooth batter. Pour into a jug or bowl.

2. Spray a large non-stick frying pan set over a medium heat with the cooking spray. Working in batches, pour tablespoons of the batter into the pan, spaced well apart as the pancakes will spread slightly. Cook until bubbles start to form on the surface, then flip the pancakes over and cook the other side for about 1 minute, until golden brown. Keep warm on a plate until all the pancakes are cooked.

SWEET POTATO and OAT PANCAKES

These freeze well and can be taken out for a quick breakfast or snack with eggs and mushrooms. They would also be a lovely starter piled with sliced smoked salmon and served with a crème fraîche and horseradish sauce.

MAKES 20 SMALL PANCAKES

250g peeled and cooked sweet potato

150g porridge oats

2 eggs, lightly beaten

1 large onion, finely chopped

1 garlic clove, finely chopped

1 tbsp finely chopped mix of fresh chives and flat-leaf parsley

500ml milk

salt and freshly ground black pepper

olive oil cooking spray

1. Mash the cooked sweet potato in a large bowl until smooth, then add the oats, eggs, onion, garlic and herbs and mix to combine, then stir in the milk to form a smooth batter. Season to taste with salt and pepper.

2. Spray a large non-stick frying pan set over a medium heat with the cooking spray. Working in batches, pour tablespoons of the batter into the pan, spaced well apart as the pancakes will spread slightly. Cook until bubbles start to form on the surface, then flip the pancakes over and cook the other side for about 1 minute, until golden brown. Keep warm on a plate until all the pancakes are cooked.

SUMMER FRUIT PANCAKES

These fat, fluffy pancakes are towards the treat end of the spectrum, so they're more suitable for a special brunch or even dessert for a posh dinner party than an everyday breakfast.

MAKES 6 PANCAKES

4 eggs, separated

50g caster sugar

2 tbsp clear honey

50g wholemeal flour

1 tbsp cornflour

For the topping:

natural yogurt or crème fraîche

fresh fruit, such as stone fruit or fresh berries

1 tbsp icing sugar

fresh mint leaves

1. Preheat the oven to 200°C. Line two large baking trays with non-stick baking paper.

2. Whisk the egg whites and sugar in a medium-sized bowl. Put the egg yolks and honey in a separate large mixing bowl and beat together, then gently fold in the egg whites. Sieve the flour and cornflour together, then gently fold these in too.

3. Spoon six mounds of batter onto the lined trays and smooth each one into a circle with the back of the spoon or spatula. Bake in the oven for 10 minutes, until cooked through and golden.

4. Leave to cool a little before removing the pancakes from the paper with a spatula and transferring to warmed plates.

5. Top with a dollop of yogurt or crème fraîche and the fruit. Dust with the icing sugar, scatter over a few fresh mint leaves and serve.

TIP:

These freeze well - just seperate each pancake with a piece of baking paper before you freeze them.

FRUIT COMPOTE

Fruit compote is lovely for breakfast served on top of porridge or yogurt. It can also be used as the base for a fruit crumble as a quick, easy and healthy dessert. To make a crumble topping, put two crispbreads (I like to use spelt and muesli ones) in a food processor with 40g of melted coconut oil and 30g of chopped nuts and pulse to combine, then tip out into a bowl and stir in 30g of porridge oats. Scatter this on top of the fruit compote in a baking dish and bake in the oven until the compote is warmed through and the topping is crisp and golden.

MAKES 20 SMALL PANCAKES

500g fruit (see the tip)

50g light brown sugar or honey

250ml water

3–4 tsp lemon juice

1. Peel and core the fruit, then cut into bite-sized pieces. Put in a heavy-based saucepan with the brown sugar or honey and the water.

2. Bring to the boil, then cover the pan and reduce to a simmer. Cook for about 10 minutes, until all the fruit is soft, then stir in the lemon juice. Remove the pan from the heat and allow to cool.

3. This will keep in a sealed container in the fridge for up to five days.

TIP:

You can use any combination of fruit, such as apples, pears and/or plums; berries and apples; pears and peaches; or rhubarb and strawberries. Just note that if you're using a soft fruit like strawberries or raspberries, you may not need to use as much water.

Try adding a cinnamon stick, a few cloves or a little vanilla extract.

You could replace the sugar or honey with some stewed dates, or try replacing the water with cider or white wine.

SAVOURY BREAKFAST MUFFINS

*These are a lifesaver when you're rushing out the door or to eat in the car – not ideal,
but sometimes needs must. They're good for lunch too with salad and a piece of fruit.
They are also a great way of sneaking vegetables into a picky child's diet.*

MAKES 12 MUFFINS

*olive oil cooking spray,
for greasing*

250g courgettes, grated

120g carrots, grated

250g wholemeal flour

125g Cheddar cheese, grated

*65g cooked or smoked
ham, chopped*

2 eggs, beaten

*120ml buttermilk or
milk kefir*

60ml sunflower oil

1 tbsp baking powder

1. Preheat the oven to 180°C. Grease a 12-hole muffin tin with the olive oil cooking spray.

2. Put the grated courgettes and carrots in a clean tea towel and squeeze hard to remove the excess water. Tip out into a large mixing bowl and add the rest of the ingredients. Mix everything together with a wooden spoon, but try to handle the ingredients lightly and don't overmix to ensure the muffins remain light.

3. Divide the batter evenly between the greased cups of the muffin tin. Bake in the oven for 25 minutes, until a skewer inserted into the middle of the muffins comes out clean.

4. Leave to rest in the tin until cool. Run a knife or spatula around the edges of each muffin to loosen it from the tin. Serve warm or cold.

TIP:

These freeze well, so you can make a big batch
in advance, perfect for lunchboxes or breakfast
on the go.

You can buy milk kefir in supermarkets or health
food shops. If you want to have a go at making
your own, you can buy kefir grains online.

DOUBLE APPLE BRAN MUFFINS

These muffins are quite filling but not too sweet, so they make a good breakfast or snack.

MAKES 12 MUFFINS

butter-flavoured cooking
spray, for greasing

100g plain flour

100g oat bran

2 tbsp flaxseeds

1 tsp baking powder

½ tsp ground cinnamon
(optional)

½ tsp fine sea salt

100g butter or coconut oil,
at room temperature

100g unsweetened apple
sauce (page 173)

75g light brown sugar

1 large egg, lightly beaten

1 Granny Smith apple,
peeled, cored and cut into
5mm cubes

1. Preheat the oven to 180°C. Line a 12-cup muffin tin
   with paper liners or lightly grease with the cooking spray.

2. Put the flour, oat bran, flaxseeds, baking powder,
   cinnamon (if using) and salt in a medium-sized bowl
   and stir to combine.

3. Put the butter or coconut oil, apple sauce, brown sugar
   and egg in a separate bowl and beat together. Fold the wet
   ingredients into the dry, taking care not to overmix, then
   fold in the apple until just combined. Divide the batter
   evenly between the greased cups of the muffin tin.

4. Bake in the oven for about 25 minutes, until the muffins
   are golden brown and the tops spring back when lightly
   touched. Allow to cool in the tin for 5 minutes, then tip out
   onto a wire rack and allow to cool completely.

5. These are best eaten on the day they're made, but they will
   keep in an airtight container for up to three days and they
   freeze well for up to three months.

PAULA'S BROWN BREAD

I've been making brown bread since I was a child. My mother baked several times a week, so for us shop-bought bread was a treat. When the snow caused the sliced pan debacle in February 2018, I just reached into the press and took out my baking box!

MAKES 1 LOAF

olive oil cooking spray, for greasing

250g plain flour

1 tsp baking powder

1 tsp bicarbonate of soda

200g porridge oats

50g oat bran

25g mixed sunflower and pumpkin seeds, plus extra for the top

1 egg

300ml buttermilk or milk kefir

2 tbsp sunflower oil

1. Preheat the oven to 200°C. Grease a 1lb loaf tin with the oil.

2. Sieve the flour, baking powder and bicarbonate of soda into a large mixing bowl, then add the porridge oats, oat bran and seeds, mixing to combine with a wooden spoon.

3. Whisk the egg in a cup, then whisk in half of the buttermilk or kefir. Put the remaining buttermilk or kefir and the sunflower oil in a separate cup and whisk those together.

4. Pour the oil and buttermilk mixture into the dry ingredients along with most of the egg mixture, reserving a little for glazing. Stir to combine – the batter will be quite wet.

5. Transfer the batter to the greased loaf tin, smoothing the top with the back of the wooden spoon. Brush the top with the remaining egg mixture and scatter with extra seeds, pushing them down a little to help them stick.

6. Bake in the oven for 35–40 minutes. Take the loaf out of the tin and tap the bottom of the loaf; if it sounds hollow, it's done. Put the loaf, out of the tin, back in the oven for 5 minutes. Allow to cool on a wire rack.

> **TIP:**
> You can buy milk kefir in supermarkets or health food shops. If you want to have a go at making your own, you can buy kefir grains online.

PORRIDGE BREAD

I nearly always have extra milk kefir in the fridge, so I often use it in cooking and baking. Heating kefir kills the beneficial bacteria in it, but even so it's a great substitute for buttermilk in this recipe. Note that different oats may need more or less liquid, so add the kefir or buttermilk slowly and mix as you go. The finished loaf is not very big, but a small slice is very tasty with a slice of cheese.

MAKES 1 LOAF

olive oil cooking spray

200g porridge oatlets, plus extra for the top

3 tbsp mixed seeds, such as chia, pumpkin, sunflower, etc., plus extra for the top

2 tsp bicarbonate of soda

½ tsp fine sea salt

325ml milk kefir or buttermilk

1 egg, lightly beaten

1 tbsp honey

1. Preheat the oven to 180°C. Spray a 2lb loaf tin generously with the cooking spray.

2. Put the dry ingredients in a large bowl and stir.

3. Put the wet ingredients in a jug and whisk to combine, then slowly add to the dry ingredients, mixing well until it's a fairly wet dough.

4. Transfer to the tin and scatter the top with the extra oats and seeds, pushing them down a little. Bake in the oven for 30 minutes, then reduce the temperature to 150°C and bake for another 30 minutes. To check that the bread is cooked, insert a skewer into the centre – it should come out clean.

5. Allow to cool in the tin on a wire rack for 10 minutes, then run a knife around the edges and tip the bread out of the tin and allow to cool completely.

TIP:

I sometimes use a sugar-free, wheat-free muesli mix from my health food shop instead of the porridge oatlets and seeds. This creates a bread that's more like a flapjack and it's absolutely gorgeous served with cheese.

You can buy milk kefir in supermarkets or health food shops. If you want to have a go at making your own, you can buy kefir grains online.

LUNCH

Lunches can be a pain. You're rushing out the door with no time to think, so you grab a banana, a yogurt and an apple. But the banana gets squashed, the yogurt is the one no one, including you, likes, plus it's out of date and the apple is bruised. You grudgingly eat it anyway but are hungry again by three o'clock, just in time for the mid-afternoon slump to hit. Lunch is the most difficult meal of the day to plan, but do make the effort to plan ahead, as a proper lunch ensures your blood sugar levels stay stable and keeps the munchies and afternoon slump at bay.

There is also the added challenge of making lunches interesting, healthy and easy to prepare. There are plenty of ready-made lunches and salads available to buy in the shops and supermarkets these days, but while they may be convenient, they also tend to be full of preservatives and lots of added sugar and salt, plus many have the salad dressing or sauce already added so that you can't control the amount yourself.

For a quick lunch idea, simply mix a handful of your favourite cooked grains with some shredded roast chicken and seasonal greens. Adding fresh herbs, spices and one of the dressings on page 97 is an easy way to add even more flavour. Grated carrots, beetroot and apple are also very good.

Use a lunchbox with compartments to carry salad, meat, salad dressing, nuts or seeds. Throw in a slice of leftover frittata (page 47, roast vegetables (page 88) or cold curry (page 170). Add a pile of washed salad leaves and a homemade dressing. Keep hard-boiled eggs in the fridge for handy snacks. Leftover noodles can be tossed with smoked mackerel, beetroot and a tangy dressing.

Armed with these quick ideas and the recipes in this chapter, you'll have no excuses now!

JOHN TOVEY'S BASIC SOUP RECIPE

John Tovey ran Miller Howe House and Restaurant in the Lake District in England, and his book was one of the first I bought on country house cooking. His recipe calls for ¼ pint of sherry but I omit that, though I sometimes add my own homemade cider, especially for the tomato and apple. I've given two variations on the basic recipe, but you could also try parsnip and mild curry; sweet potato and tinned coconut milk; or any other combination of vegetables and flavours that appeals to you.

SERVES 6

Basic version:

1 tbsp rapeseed oil

900g prepared vegetables, such as carrots, parsnips, sweet potato or butternut squash

200g onion, chopped

1 litre vegetable stock

Carrot and ginger version:

900g carrots, chopped

200g onion, chopped

25g fresh ginger, peeled and finely chopped

1.3 litres vegetable stock

Tomato and apple version:

1 tbsp rapeseed oil

450g ripe tomatoes, peeled and chopped

450g red apples, peeled, cored and chopped

200g onion, chopped

1.1 litres vegetable stock

200ml dry cider

1½ tbsp apple cider vinegar (optional), added at the end

1. Heat the oil in a large heavy-based saucepan or pot over a medium heat. Add the vegetables and onion (and the ginger for the carrot and ginger soup) and cook for a few minutes. Dampen a sheet of greaseproof paper and cover the vegetable mix snugly, then cover the pan with a lid and simmer over a low heat for 40–45 minutes, until the veg are completely softened.

2. Add the stock (and cider if making the tomato and apple soup), then blend until smooth with a hand-held blender or in a food processor. If making the tomato and apple soup, stir in the apple cider vinegar at the very end (if using).

> **TIP:**
>
> I use the vegan Marigold bouillon powder. It's widely available and low in salt too.

CHICKEN NOODLE SOUP

It's a wet and windy March day. The hens are complaining as they hate getting wet, even though they got a bucket of scraps mixed with oats and hot water just now. I'm cold and hungry after my excursion to the henhouse and want a nice comforting lunch that's guilt free and filling. This chicken noodle soup will hit the spot, plus it's quick and easy to make: comfort in a bowl.

You don't need to start with raw chicken if you have leftovers from a roast dinner, or you could pick up a pack of cooked chicken in the supermarket. You could also buy a jar each of ginger paste and garlic paste at your local Asian shop (where it will be much cheaper than the tubes you buy in the supermarket) and a pack of spiralized vegetables like courgettes or a pack of medium noodles.

SERVES 4

900ml spicy chicken broth (page 112) or chicken stock

8 mushrooms, thinly sliced

4 spring onions, chopped (keep the green tops for garnish)

2 garlic cloves, finely chopped, or 2 tsp garlic paste

1 heaped tsp chopped fresh ginger or ginger paste

300g chopped cooked chicken

2 medium courgettes, spiralized

freshly ground black pepper

sweet chilli sauce (optional)

tamari or soy sauce (optional)

1. Pour the broth or stock into a large saucepan and bring to the boil. Add the mushrooms, spring onions, garlic and ginger. Cook on a low heat for 5–10 minutes to allow the flavours to blend together.

2. Add the chicken and allow it to heat through, then add the spiralized courgettes and allow to just heat through, not cook. Taste and add black pepper, sweet chilli sauce and tamari or soy sauce to your liking (if using).

3. Ladle into warmed bowls and sprinkle with the reserved chopped green tops of the spring onions.

TIP:
Tamari is a gluten-free dark soy sauce.

SPICY VEGETABLE AND LENTIL SOUP

This is a hearty winter soup that will bring comfort on a dark and dreary day. I did this recipe for a radio programme where I visited people's homes and encouraged them to cook fresh food. The lady on the day didn't know much about cooking with spices and was intrigued by how good this soup was.

SERVES 4–6

1 tbsp sunflower oil

1 large onion, chopped

2 garlic cloves, chopped

2 tsp ground cumin

1 heaped tsp ground turmeric

1 tsp ground cardamom

2 large carrots, diced into small pieces

1 parsnip, diced into small pieces

¼ celeriac (approx. 150g), diced into small pieces

150g ready-cooked or tinned green lentils

1 litre vegetable stock

120g green cabbage, thinly sliced (optional)

salt and freshly ground black pepper

1. Heat the oil in a large heavy-based saucepan over a medium heat. Add the onion, garlic and spices and fry gently for 4 minutes, until the spices are fragrant.

2. Add the remaining vegetables, lentils and stock. Bring to the boil, then reduce the heat and simmer gently until the vegetables are cooked to your liking.

3. Season to taste with salt and pepper, then ladle into warmed bowls to serve.

> **TIP:**
>
> I use the vegan Marigold stock powder. It's widely available and low in salt too.
>
> Add chopped cooked chicken or ham to make this a hearty main course. If using cabbage, add it before the chicken or ham and cook until tender.

PARSNIP, SAGE and WHITE BEAN SOUP

Sage is sometimes called the women's herb; it's good for menstrual and menopausal symptoms. In mediaeval times, if a woman couldn't grow sage, she was not considered the boss of the house!

SERVES 4–6

olive oil cooking spray

2 large parsnips, roughly chopped (see the tip for what to do with the peelings)

1 onion, roughly chopped

1 x 400g tin of cannellini beans, drained and rinsed

1 litre vegetable stock, plus extra if needed

1 sprig of fresh sage, roughly chopped, plus extra to garnish

1 fresh bay leaf

1. Spray a large heavy-based saucepan set over a medium heat with the oil. Add the parsnips and onion, cover the pan and sweat for 10 minutes, until softened but not coloured.

2. Add the beans (or keep back some of the whole beans and add them at the end for extra texture), stock, sage and bay leaf. Bring to the boil, then reduce the heat and simmer for 15 minutes.

3. Remove the bay leaf, then blitz the soup with a hand-held blender until smooth. Add a little more stock or water if the soup is too thick.

4. To serve, ladle the soup into warmed bowls and garnish with the extra sage.

TIP:

Spray the reserved parsnip peelings with oil, scatter on a baking tray in an even layer and bake in an oven preheated to 200°C for 10 minutes, until crisp. Use to garnish the soup. I use the vegan Marigold stock powder. It's widely available and low in salt too.

Most people use sage once a year for their holiday stuffing, but it has many other delicious uses, particularly with pork, beans, potatoes, cheese and in sage and brown butter sauce. The flavour can be intense, so start with a small amount and build on that.

CARROT and TAHINI SOUP

I make hummus all the time (see my recipe on page 188), so I always have tahini in the press. This soup is velvety and delicious and is a nice change from the usual carrot and ginger.

SERVES 4–6

olive oil cooking spray

1 large onion, finely chopped

2 garlic cloves, finely chopped

½ tsp ground coriander

½ tsp ground turmeric

½ tsp freshly ground black pepper

a pinch of cayenne pepper

600g carrots, chopped

900ml vegetable stock

a few sprigs of fresh thyme

75g light tahini

salt

a handful of chopped fresh coriander or mint, to garnish

1. Spray a large heavy-based saucepan set over a medium heat with the oil. When it's hot, add the onion and garlic, cover the pan and cook for 4 minutes, until softened but not coloured. Reduce the heat to low, then add all the spices and cook for 3 minutes. Add the carrots and cover the pan. Cook for 10 minutes, until the carrots are soft. Add a little stock if necessary to prevent the veg burning.

2. Add the remaining stock and the thyme. Bring to the boil, then reduce the heat and simmer for 10 minutes. Stir in the tahini.

3. Remove the pan from the heat, then remove and discard the thyme sprigs. Purée the soup with a hand-held blender until smooth. Season to taste with salt and pepper.

4. To serve, ladle the soup into warmed bowls and garnish with a little chopped fresh coriander or mint.

> **TIP:**
>
> I use the vegan Marigold stock powder. It's widely available and low in salt too.

WHITE ONION and THYME SOUP

We make this in the summer, when we have our own onions and thyme growing in the garden. It's a big hit with our guests and is sophisticated enough for a dinner party served with some breadsticks on the side.

SERVES 6

1 tbsp rapeseed oil

1.1kg white onions, sliced

1 tbsp fresh thyme leaves, plus extra to garnish

1.2 litres vegetable stock

salt and freshly ground black pepper

freshly grated Parmesan cheese, to garnish

1. Heat the oil in a large heavy-based saucepan over a medium heat. When the oil is hot, add the onions and thyme. Dampen a sheet of greaseproof paper and cover the onions snugly, then cover the pan with a lid and simmer over a low heat for 40–45 minutes, until completely softened. Sweating the onions like this brings out their flavour.

2. Remove the paper, then pour in the stock. Purée the soup with a hand-held blender until smooth, then season to taste with salt and pepper.

3. To serve, ladle the soup into warmed bowls and garnish with a pinch of grated Parmesan.

> **TIP:**
>
> The onions are the star of this soup, so use organic ones for the best flavour.
>
> I use the vegan Marigold stock powder. It's widely available and low in salt too.

WARM SMOKED MACKEREL SALAD

We don't eat a lot of fish in Ireland and it can be difficult to get really fresh fish. People don't like cooking it as it can break up in the pan, but quickly pan-frying the smoked mackerel is effortless.

SERVES 2

2 tsp sunflower seeds

2 smoked mackerel fillets, skinned

a large handful of baby spinach

lime wedges, to serve

For the dressing:

75ml buttermilk or milk kefir

1 tsp Dijon mustard

1 tsp wholegrain mustard

1 tbsp chopped fresh dill

salt and freshly ground black pepper

1. First make the dressing. Put the buttermilk or milk kefir and the two types of mustard in a jar, screw on the lid and shake well, then add the chopped dill. Taste and season with salt and pepper.

2. To toast the sunflower seeds, put a non-stick frying pan on a medium heat. Add the seeds to the hot pan and cook for 3–4 minutes, tossing occasionally, until golden brown. Tip out into a bowl and set aside.

3. Raise the heat to high, then add the mackerel fillets, flesh side down, and sear for 2–3 minutes. Searing the mackerel like this makes it more tasty and less oily.

4. Divide the baby spinach between two plates, then scatter over the toasted sunflower seeds. Drizzle over the dressing, then place the seared mackerel on the side. Serve with a wedge of lime.

TIP:

The red apple, beetroot and celeriac slaw on page 100 goes wonderfully with this.

You can buy milk kefir in supermarkets or health food shops. If you want to have a go at making your own, you can buy kefir grains online.

SMOKED MACKEREL HOT POTS

For some reason, this Reveries dish was especially popular with men. My son Paul loves this as a starter when he comes home for a roast beef lunch.

SERVES 4–6

olive oil cooking spray

1 small onion, finely chopped

1 small fennel bulb, finely chopped (save the fronds for garnish)

2 celery sticks, shaved and finely chopped (see the tip)

1 spring onion, finely chopped

260g smoked mackerel or hot smoked salmon, skinned

2 ripe tomatoes, chopped

juice of ½ lemon

2 tbsp crème fraîche

freshly ground black pepper

1 crispbread

2 tbsp grated Parmesan cheese

1. Preheat the oven to 180°C.

2. Spray a non-stick frying pan set over a medium heat with a little oil. Add the onion, fennel, celery and spring onion. Cover the pan with a lid and sweat the veg for about 4 minutes, until they're almost soft. Remove the pan from the heat and set aside, uncovered, to cool.

3. Flake the smoked mackerel or salmon into a large bowl. Add the tomatoes, lemon juice and crème fraîche and season with freshly ground black pepper. Add the lightly cooked vegetables and gently mix everything together. Divide between four to six ramekins or put in a medium-sized baking dish.

4. Put the crispbread in a ziplock bag and use a rolling pin to bash it into crumbs. Scatter the crispbread crumbs evenly between the ramekins or over the baking dish, followed by the grated Parmesan.

5. Bake in the oven for 20 minutes, until nicely browned on top. Garnish with the reserved fennel fronds.

> **TIP:**
> Always shave your celery with a vegetable peeler, no matter what dish you're using it in – it's far nicer when you get rid of its stringiness.

COURGETTI and FETA SALAD

The best vegetables and fruit to spiralize and eat raw are courgettes, cucumbers, beetroot, carrots, apples and melon. Spiralized apple and melon make a delicious, refreshing snack, while cucumber or carrot add crunch to salads. Sweet potatoes and butternut squash are also fun to spiralize, but they need to be cooked lightly first. Courgetti keep well in an airtight container in the fridge for a few days, so make a big batch to use for a few days' worth of lunches.

SERVES 2

1 large or 2 small courgettes, spiralized

2 ripe tomatoes, chopped

100g feta cheese, crumbled

handful of toasted sesame seeds (see the tip)

1–2 tbsp oil-free dressing (page 97)

salt and freshly ground black pepper

1. This couldn't be easier to make – simply put the courgettes, tomatoes, feta, sesame seeds and dressing in a large bowl and toss together, then season to taste with salt and pepper. Divide between two large shallow bowls and serve straight away.

TIP:

If you don't have a spiralizer, you can buy packs of spiralized courgettes and other vegetables in most supermarkets. Alternatively use a vegetable peeler to shave the courgettes into ribbons.

To toast the sesame seeds, put a non-stick frying pan on a gentle heat without any oil. Add the seeds and cook, stirring frequently just until they turn golden brown, then tip out onto a plate.

CHICKPEA and FREEKEH SALAD

Freekeh is an ancient grain made from green durum wheat that is roasted and rubbed to create its distinct flavour. It's similar to barley or couscous, but nuttier.

SERVES 4

360ml water

60g freekeh

1 x 400g tin of chickpeas, drained and rinsed

85g feta cheese, cubed

55g salami, chopped

1 ripe avocado, halved, stoned, peeled and cubed or sliced

1 garlic clove, crushed

1 tbsp olive oil

a handful of chopped fresh mint

a handful of chopped fresh flat-leaf parsley

salt and freshly ground black pepper

1. Pour the water into a medium saucepan and bring to the boil, then add the freekeh. Bring back to the boil, then reduce the heat, cover the pan and cook for 20 minutes, until most of the water has been absorbed and the freekeh is tender. Put the freekeh in a sieve and run under cold water to cool it down quickly. Drain well and set aside.

2. Put the chickpeas, feta, salami, avocado and garlic in a bowl. Drizzle with the oil and toss lightly to coat, then stir in the freekeh and herbs. Season to taste with salt and pepper.

3. Serve immediately or cover and chill in the fridge for up to 4 hours.

RED APPLE, BEETROOT AND CELERIAC SLAW

This is a favourite salad of mine for our American guests, who always ask me to share the recipe. The celeriac has a strong celery-like taste that works really well in this slaw. If you're preparing this salad ahead of time, add the beetroot at the last minute so that the colours stay separate, otherwise it will make the entire dish pink.

SERVES 4

2 tbsp apple juice

80g celeriac, peeled

1 red apple, halved and cored (leave the skin on)

1 fresh beetroot, peeled

1 tbsp chopped fresh chives

1. Put the apple juice in a large bowl. Grate the celeriac, apple and beetroot into the bowl, in that order. Stir well, then add the chives and stir once more to combine.

TIP:

To make this more of a salad than a slaw, you could spiralize the vegetables instead of grating them and drizzle with 1½ tablespoons of maple dressing (page 97).

Use disposable gloves when handling the beetroot so that your hands don't get stained.

COURGETTI with FRESH TOMATO SAUCE

Spiralized courgette 'noodles', or courgetti, have become a popular substitute for spaghetti and are a great way of making dishes lighter and more nutritious.

SERVES 4

2 tbsp olive oil

4 large ripe tomatoes, chopped

2 medium courgettes, spiralized

1 bunch of fresh basil, chopped or torn

salt and freshly ground black pepper

grated Parmesan cheese or crumbled feta cheese, to serve

a few basil leaves, to serve

1. Heat the oil in a large non-stick frying pan over a medium heat. Add the tomatoes and cook for 3–4 minutes, until they're just starting to break down but still retain their shape. Add the spiralized courgettes and allow to just heat through. Stir in the basil and season to taste.

2. To serve, divide the courgetti and tomato sauce between four wide, shallow bowls and scatter with some grated Parmesan or crumbled feta cheese and some basil leaves.

TIP:

If you don't have a spiralizer, you can buy packs of spiralized courgettes and other vegetables in most supermarkets.

DINNER

By six o'clock you will likely have arrived home after a busy day. How you feel will depend on your day, but it will also depend on what and when you have eaten during the day. If you have breakfasted and lunched well, had a healthy snack and drunk enough water, your blood sugar levels will be steady and you will be able to look forward to preparing a nice dinner.

The recipes in this chapter are nearly all quick and easy to prepare and all are tasty and healthy. Many freeze well or can be partly prepared in advance. Just plan ahead and know what you will be eating. Leaving it to chance increases the risk of you choosing a takeaway or some other easy, unhealthy option.

Remember to keep an eye on your portion sizes. Your plate should be one-quarter protein (a fist-sized portion), one-quarter carbohydrate and the remaining half should be salad or vegetables. It also helps to use a smaller plate. Dinner plates nowadays can be as big as 30cm, whereas when I was a child they were 24cm.

Eat slowly and leave your knife and fork down in between mouthfuls (I find this very hard to do!). There is a sound scientific reason for this: your stomach is slow to realise it's full and thus release the hormones that help control your eating, so eating slowly gives it a chance to send those signals before you go too far. Protein and fibre take more time to be digested, so they help to regulate your blood sugar levels and prevent the energy slump.

Above all else, enjoy your dinner. Set the table, turn off the TV, relax and chat with your family. Or if you live alone, do what my mother-in-law does and set the table with a nice placemat, cutlery and crockery, cook a nice meal, sit down to enjoy it and treat yourself like a VIP.

POACHED WHOLE CHICKEN in SPICY BROTH

I did three Saturdays of cooking demonstrations in my house last January and this recipe was a big hit. The chicken is moist and full of flavour and the stock is super rich. My students reminisced about mothers and grandmothers who always cooked chicken like this and made a white chicken stew with carrots and potatoes.

SERVES 4–6

200g chestnut, shiitake or button mushrooms, sliced

1 onion, finely chopped

4 garlic cloves, peeled but left whole

2 fresh red chillies, halved and deseeded (optional; see the tip)

a thumb-sized piece of fresh ginger

2 star anise

1 cinnamon stick

1.5 litres water

2 tbsp soy sauce (use tamari or a light soy sauce for less salt)

2 tbsp oyster sauce, plus extra to serve

1 x 1.6kg free-range chicken

1. Put all the ingredients except the chicken in a large saucepan over a high heat. Cover and bring to the boil, then add the whole chicken, breast side down. Cover with the lid and bring back to the boil, then reduce the heat and simmer for 40–45 minutes, until the chicken is cooked through. Use a meat thermometer to check that the internal heat is at least 75°C. Be sure you insert the thermometer in the thickest part of the leg, not touching the bone.

2. Carefully remove the chicken and allow it to cool slightly. When it's cool enough to handle, carve the breasts from the chicken and shred the meat from the legs and the rest of the carcass. (Plastic kitchen gloves make this a nicer job!)

3. Strain the broth into a large bowl and allow it to cool. You can reuse the star anise and cinnamon if you pick them out of the broth, rinse them and pat them dry. Discard the remaining solids.

4. To serve, reheat the broth and shredded chicken in a clean saucepan, then ladle into warmed bowls. Drizzle with extra oyster sauce or put a little sauce in a small bowl and allow everyone to help themselves.

TIP:

This poached chicken and its spicy broth will give you the base for several other dishes, such as the chicken noodle soup on page 74.

Not everyone likes chillies, so leave them out if desired.

JOLLOF RICE with CHICKEN

Since I retired from the public health service, I have volunteered at Globe House. I used to serve as a medical officer for the asylum seekers who live there. In a nearby polytunnel, the residents grow vegetables, herbs and lots of chillies. We have regular cooking days, when eight or more of us cram into the tiny residents' kitchen. It's an international gathering of cooks from Bangladesh, Afghanistan and Nigeria. Naomi and I are the willing helpers/students.

SERVES 6

400g long-grain rice

2 x 400g tins of whole plum tomatoes

1 onion, halved and sliced

1 red pepper, deseeded and thickly sliced

1 yellow pepper, deseeded and thickly sliced

2 garlic cloves, chopped

1 Scotch bonnet chilli, deseeded (optional; see the tip)

a thumb-sized piece of fresh ginger, peeled and chopped

3 tbsp tomato purée

1 chicken stock cube or 1 teaspoon Marigold bouillon

600ml just-boiled water

8 skinless, boneless chicken thighs, cut into large pieces

1 bunch of fresh coriander, roughly chopped

1. Fill the kettle and boil the water. Put the rice into a large heatproof bowl, cover with the just-boiled water and leave for 20 minutes.

2. Meanwhile, put the tomatoes, onion, peppers, garlic, chilli (if using) and ginger in a food processor or blender and whizz until smooth.

3. Pour the purée into large sauté pan over a medium heat and let it cook for a few minutes. Stir in the tomato purée, then add the stock cube or powder and pour in 600ml of just-boiled water. Add the chicken and bring to the boil, then reduce the heat and simmer for 15 minutes.

4. Strain the rice and add it to the pan. Cover the pan with foil or a lid so that no steam can escape, then cook for 20 minutes.

5. To serve, ladle the jollof rice and chicken into warmed shallow bowls and garnish with the chopped fresh coriander.

> **TIP:**
> Basmati rice isn't suitable for this recipe.
> I sometimes omit the chilli but add a pinch of cayenne pepper to the purée.
>
> I use the vegan Marigold bouillon powder. It's widely available and low in salt too.

CHICKEN MARENGO

The first cookbook that Damien bought me was by Robert Carrier, who was a TV star in the 1980s. I grew up in a house where garlic was never used, as my father only ate good plain food, so this recipe felt very exotic to me at the time!

SERVES 2

olive oil cooking spray

4 skinless chicken legs

300g button mushrooms, halved

1 x 500g jar of garlic and herb passata

1 chicken stock cube

a pinch of freshly ground black pepper

chopped fresh flat-leaf parsley, to garnish

green salad, pasta, baby potatoes or green veg (optional), to serve

1. Heat five spritzes of the oil in a large casserole or heavy-based pan over a medium-high heat. Add the chicken legs and cook briefly on each side to colour them a little, then transfer to a plate. Add the mushrooms and fry for about 5 minutes, until they start to soften.

2. Pour in the passata and crumble in the stock cube. Season with black pepper – you shouldn't need salt because the stock cube probably has plenty. Add the chicken legs back to the casserole or pan, then cover, reduce the heat to medium-low and simmer for 40 minutes, until the chicken is completely cooked through.

3. Garnish with the chopped fresh parsley and serve with a green salad, pasta, baby potatoes or green veg, if you like.

CHICKEN THIGHS with HONEY and MUSTARD

This is a quick dinner dish, but the chicken is also good cold in a salad or chopped and used to fill an aubergine roll (page 109) with some hummus (page 188) and lettuce.

SERVES 4

8 skinless chicken thighs

2 tbsp wholegrain mustard

½ tbsp honey

salt and freshly ground black pepper

100g crème fraîche

chopped fresh flat-leaf parsley, to garnish

1. Preheat the oven to 190°C.

2. Put the chicken thighs on a baking tray. Mix the mustard and honey together in a small bowl, then use a pastry brush to coat the chicken thighs with the mixture. Season with salt and pepper.

3. Cook in the oven for 25–30 minutes, until the chicken is completely cooked through.

4. Remove the thighs to a serving dish and pour the juices from the baking tray into a pan. Add the crème fraîche and bring to the boil. Pour the sauce over the chicken, garnish with some parsley and serve straight away.

TIP:

Make a meal out of this by serving the chicken with boiled baby potatoes, steamed carrots and wilted spinach

CHICKEN with RAS EL HANOUT and BEETROOT

I can't tolerate chilli, which encourages me to experiment with other spice mixes. Ras el hanout is a Persian mix of turmeric, fenugreek, caraway, coriander, cumin, cayenne and black pepper. It's a surprisingly versatile spice that works really well with chicken or lamb and adds a lovely flavour to the beetroot here.

This is one of those easy dishes that you could prepare in the morning and put in the fridge for the day, leaving you with nothing to do when you get home except put it in the oven.

SERVES 4

3–4 red onions

8 boneless, skinless chicken thighs

1 large beetroot, peeled and cut into wedges

olive oil cooking spray

2 tbsp ras el hanout

salt and freshly ground black pepper

Greek yogurt, to serve

1. Preheat the oven to 200°C.

2. Cut the onions into quarters through the root end, leaving the root intact so that the quarters stay together and don't fall apart.

3. Put the onions, chicken thighs and beetroot on a large baking tray and spread them out in an even layer. Spray with five spritzes of the olive oil, then sprinkle over the ras el hanout and season with salt and pepper.

4. Cook in the oven for 35 minutes, until the chicken is completely cooked through. Serve with a dollop of Greek yogurt on top.

> **TIP:**
>
> Ras el hanout is widely available in supermarkets, but it can also be found in your local Asian market.
>
> Boned chicken thighs are sometimes called oyster thighs, so keep your eye out for them on the supermarket shelves.

DUCK BREASTS with ORANGE and GINGER SAUCE

Duck meat can be very dry if you cook it without the skin and fat, so I remove them after cooking. The trick to getting the skin really crisp is to leave it uncovered in the fridge overnight, then put it under an electric fan (if you have one); otherwise leave it in the fridge until ready to cook. Score the skin and fat before cooking.

SERVES 2 OR MORE

2 x 175g duck breasts

juice of 1 large orange or 100ml good-quality orange juice

1 tsp ginger purée

2 tsp plum sauce or plum conserve

1 ripe plum, stoned and halved

wilted pak choi, to serve

boiled basmati rice or udon noodles, to serve

1. Heat a heavy-based non-stick frying pan on a very high heat until smoking hot. Don't add any oil to the pan.

2. Using a sharp knife, score the skin and fat on the duck breasts. Add to the pan, skin side down, and cook for 5 minutes without moving them so that they brown well. Working very carefully (wear oven gloves), frequently pour the excess fat into a dish. Once the skin is golden brown, turn the breasts over and sear the other side for 5 minutes, until browned.

3. Transfer the duck to a rack set in a baking tray or roasting tin. Put the tray in the oven and cook for 10 minutes for medium rare or 15 minutes for well done. Allow the meat to rest for 10 minutes before carving.

4. To make the sauce, wipe out the pan, add the orange juice and ginger and bring to the boil. Allow it to bubble down to reduce, then stir in the plum sauce or conserve.

5. Add the halved plums to the pan you cooked the sauce in, cut side down. Cook over a medium-high heat for a few minutes without touching them, until they're nicely caramelised.

6. To serve, carve the duck into thin slices and drizzle the sauce over each portion. Serve with a caramelised plum half, lightly wilted pak choi and basmati rice or udon noodles.

> **TIP:**
>
> You can find plum sauce in Asian markets.
>
> Use any leftover duck to fill an omelette wrap (page 46) for lunch the next day

HEALTHY BEEF CASSEROLE

The trick to getting a rich flavour is browning the meat properly.

SERVES 6

olive oil cooking spray

1.35kg stewing beef or shin of beef, cut into 5cm chunks (see also the tip)

apple cider, red wine or white wine vinegar (optional), to deglaze the pan

225g carrots, peeled and cut into 5cm chunks

225g celery, cut into 5cm chunks

4 sprigs fresh thyme

1 bay leaf

1½ tsp fine sea salt

freshly ground black pepper

725ml dry cider or vegetable stock

1 tbsp Worcestershire sauce

1 x 400g tin of butter beans, drained and rinsed

1. Preheat the oven to 160°C.

2. Lightly spray a large non-stick frying pan with the oil and set the pan over a high heat. Brown the meat in batches, keeping the chunks spaced well apart to avoid stewing the meat.

3. Between batches, add a little water to the pan, bring it to the boil and use a wooden spatula to scrape up the brown bits to deglaze the pan. You could also add 1 tablespoon of apple cider, red wine or white wine vinegar to the pan, boil it until it disappears, then add a splash of water and let it bubble up again. As the meat is browned, add it and the deglazed juices to a 3.5-litre casserole with a tight-fitting lid. Lightly spray the pan with oil again and allow it to come back up to a high heat before adding the next batch of beef and repeating the deglazing process.

4. Once all the beef is in the casserole, add the carrots and celery to the casserole along with the herbs, salt and pepper, then pour in the cider or stock and the Worcestershire sauce. Put the casserole on the hob and bring it up to a gentle simmer.

5. Cover the casserole with a sheet of foil, then a tight-fitting lid. Put the casserole on the middle shelf of the oven and cook for 2½–3 hours, until the beef is completely tender.

6. Remove the casserole from the oven and raise the temperature to 200°C. Stir well, then add the butter beans.

7. Return the casserole to the oven and cook, uncovered, for a further 25–30 minutes, to reduce and thicken the juices. Ladle into warmed shallow bowls to serve.

BEEF BULGOGI

My son Paul is always hovering around the kitchen island, checking out what's for dinner. Beef bulgogi, or Korean-style beef, is one of his favourites. You can use any vegetables you like.

SERVES 4

450g beef sirloin

1 small, firm pear, unpeeled and grated

1 small apple, unpeeled and grated, or 1 tbsp apple juice

2 garlic cloves, grated or crushed

3 tbsp dark brown sugar (or equivalent sweetener)

3 tbsp tamari or soy sauce

1½ tbsp toasted sesame or olive oil

1½ tsp grated fresh ginger

1 small onion, grated

1 small carrot, julienned

4 button mushrooms, sliced

4 fresh chives, snipped, to garnish

1 tbsp black sesame seeds, to garnish

1 tbsp toasted white sesame seeds, to garnish (see the tip)

1. Wrap the steak in cling film and place in the freezer for 20 minutes. Remove the film and slice the beef very thinly.

2. In a large bowl, mix together the pear, apple, garlic, sugar, tamari or soy sauce, oil and ginger. Add the beef, mix well, cover and leave to sit for 30 minutes at room temperature or in the fridge overnight.

3. Heat a large non-stick frying pan or wok over a medium-high heat. Use tongs to lift each piece of beef out of the marinade, shaking off any excess. Retain the marinade. Working in batches so that you don't crowd the pan, dry-fry the beef for 4–5 minutes, stirring occasionally, until the meat is browned. Transfer the cooked beef to a dish. Once all the beef is cooked, return it all to the pan.

4. Add the vegetables and cook for 5 minutes, until slightly softened. Raise the heat to high, add the retained marinade and cook for 4–5 minutes, stirring occasionally, until the marinade has reduced and the veg are cooked.

5. Transfer the beef and vegetables to a serving platter, then garnish with the chives and sesame seeds.

> **TIP:**
>
> This recipe works equally well with pork, chicken, lamb or venison.
>
> If you're in a rush, make a lazy version: substitute 2 tablespoons of apple juice for the pear and apple; use 1 teaspoon of garlic paste and 1 teaspoon of ginger purée instead of the fresh garlic and ginger and leave out the grated onion.

SHREDDED FIVE-SPICE PORK

Damien loves five-spice – a mix of star anise, Szechuan peppercorns, fennel, cinnamon and cloves that adds sweetness and depth to savoury dishes, especially beef, duck and pork. I often make this for a quick, healthy dinner with a pack of pre-cooked brown rice and some sautéed pak choi.

SERVES 4–6

450g lean pork (see the tip)

1 garlic clove, crushed

1 tbsp dark soy sauce

½ tsp five-spice powder

½ tsp grated fresh ginger

2 tbsp peanut oil or 10 spritzes of olive oil cooking spray

4 tbsp stock or water

2 tsp arrowroot powder

4 tbsp water

brown rice or noodles, to serve

green veg, to serve

1. Wrap the pork in cling film, then put it in the freezer for 20 minutes. Remove the cling film, then use a sharp knife to slice it as thinly as possible.

2. Put the garlic, soy sauce, five-spice power and ginger in a medium-sized bowl. Add the pork and toss to coat. Cover the bowl with cling film and marinate in the fridge for 1 hour.

3. Heat the oil in a non-stick wok or large frying pan over a high heat until it's smoking hot. Working in small batches, add the shredded pork to the hot wok or pan and cook until it's crisp and brown. Keep warm in a side dish until all the pork has been cooked.

4. Reduce the heat, then return all the pork to the wok or pan and add the stock. Blend the arrowroot with the water in a small bowl, then sprinkle this over the pork, stirring well so that it blends into the dish.

5. Serve with brown rice or noodles and accompany with a green veg on the side.

TIP:

Look for packs of stir-fry pork strips in the supermarket, but you can use pork chops or fillet too.

This works just as well with beef or chicken.

MOROCCAN LAMB TAGINE

SERVES 4–6

1 tbsp ground turmeric

2 tsp each ground cinnamon
and freshly ground black pepper

1½ tsp each paprika
and ground ginger

1 tsp cayenne pepper

1kg shoulder of lamb, diced
into 5cm cubes

olive oil cooking spray

2 large onions, chopped

3 garlic cloves, crushed

600ml vegetable stock

500ml tomato passata

2 x 400g tins of chopped tomatoes

85g flaked almonds,
plus extra to garnish

115g dried apricots, halved

55g dates, pitted and halved

55g golden sultanas

1 tsp saffron soaked in water

1 tsp honey

salt and freshly ground
black pepper

couscous or rice, to serve

1. Mix all the spices in a small bowl. Put the lamb in a large bowl and add half of the spices, tossing to coat. Cover the bowl with cling film and put the lamb in the fridge overnight.

2. Preheat the oven to 150°C.

3. Spray a large casserole with the oil and set over a medium heat. Add the onion, garlic and the remaining spices and cook for 5 minutes, until soft.

4. Meanwhile, spray a large frying pan over a high heat with the oil. Working in batches so that you don't crowd the pan, add the lamb and cook until it's browned on all sides, then transfer to the casserole. Deglaze the pan in between batches with some of the vegetable stock, then add the stock and any browned bits from the pan to the casserole too.

5. Once all the lamb has been browned and added to the casserole, add all of the remaining ingredients and the remaining stock and season to taste with salt and pepper. Cover the casserole tightly with the lid and cook in the oven for 2½ hours, until the lamb is completely tender.

6. To serve, put some couscous or rice in wide, shallow bowls, then ladle the lamb tagine on top and garnish with the extra flaked almonds and some flat-leaf parsley, if desired.

> **TIP:**
> The red apple, beetroot and celeriac slaw on page 100 would go well with the tagine as a side dish, as would a mix of chopped ripe tomatoes and baby radishes.

VIETNAMESE LAMB CUPS

This is a really fast, easy supper dish. You could add some cooked grains, defrosted peas, tinned sweetcorn and chopped fresh parsley for a slightly more filling version.

SERVES 4

500g lamb mince

zest and juice of 2 limes, plus lime wedges to serve

2 tbsp fish sauce

½ tbsp light brown sugar

1 tbsp rice wine vinegar (or white wine vinegar or apple cider vinegar)

2 spring onions, thinly sliced

a small handful of fresh mint leaves, chopped

¼ tsp cayenne pepper, to taste; or deseeded finely sliced fresh chillies, to taste

2 heads of Little Gem lettuce, leaves separated

40g roasted peanuts

1. Put a non-stick wok or a large pan over a high heat with no oil until it's smoking hot. Working in batches, add the mince and dry-fry for 5 minutes, regularly pouring off any fat that renders out. Use a slotted spoon to transfer the browned meat to a plate and continue until all the lamb is cooked.

2. Use tongs to wipe out the wok or pan with kitchen paper. Put all the browned lamb mince back in the wok or pan, then add the lime zest and juice, fish sauce, brown sugar and vinegar and fry for 2–3 minutes, until the mince is sticky and golden. Stir in the spring onions, most of the mint and the cayenne pepper or chillies. Check the seasoning, then tip into a warm serving bowl and take to the table.

3. Put the individual lettuce leaves on a serving platter. Put the reserved mint leaves, peanuts and lime wedges in separate small bowls. Let everyone fill the lettuce cups with the lamb and garnish as they like.

> **TIP:**
>
> Lean beef mince works just as well in this recipe.
>
> If you have the patience for lots of batch frying you could scale this up for a buffet dish for a party or event. Once cooled, the cooked lamb mince will keep in the fridge in an airtight container for up to three days.

SPEEDY FISH SUPPER

Using the microwave to cook fish is handy, but always check your cooking time, as it may take less than you think. The fish needs to be an even thickness, so tuck under the thin edge of the fillet if needed and have the thicker end at the outer edge. Check it after 3 minutes, then leave to rest for 30 seconds and finish in 90-second bursts to ensure you don't overcook the fish.

SERVES 2

1 x 400g tin of cannellini beans, drained and rinsed

100g dry-cured chorizo, chopped into small chunks

1 handful of fresh dill, stalks removed and finely chopped

1 tbsp olive oil

1 tsp lemon or lime juice

2 x 175g skinless white fish fillets, such as cod

salt and freshly ground black pepper

garden peas, to serve

1. Tip the beans, chorizo and most of the dill into a shallow microwave-proof dish. Stir in half the oil and the lemon or lime juice. Top with the fish fillets and drizzle with the remaining oil, then season with salt and pepper.

2. Cover the dish with cling film and pierce it a few times. Microwave on high for 4–5 minutes (check after 3 minutes – see the intro), until the fish looks opaque and flakes easily.

3. Remove the fish from the dish. Stir together the beans and chorizo, then spoon onto two warmed plates. Top with the fish and scatter with the remaining dill. Serve with garden peas on the side.

TIP:

For an extra boost of flavour, toss the asparagus or broccoli with some of the lemon ginger dressing on page 97.

BEET BURGERS

These are a great vegetarian option. I make a big batch and freeze them for up to a month.

MAKES 4

olive oil cooking spray

1 red onion, finely chopped

2 garlic cloves, crushed

1 tsp ras el hanout

100g crispbread

180g cooked and cooled
brown rice or other grain

130g tinned green lentils,
drained and rinsed

130g raw beetroot, peeled
and grated

2 tbsp smooth almond or
peanut butter

½ tsp fine sea salt

creosa sauce (page 178),
to serve

1. Spray a non-stick frying pan with oil and set the pan over a medium heat. **Add** the onion and cook for 5 minutes, until soft. Add the **garlic** and **ras** el hanout and cook gently for 3 minutes. Remove the pan from the heat and allow to cool.

2. Put the crispbread in a food processor and blitz until it forms fine crumbs. **Transfer** to a bowl and mix in the cooked onion mixture along **with** the cooked rice or grain, lentils, grated beetroot, nut **butter** and salt. Form into six burgers using a burger mould **or use** a ring mould to give them a nice shape. Put the burgers **on** a plate, cover with cling film and chill in the fridge for **at least** 15 minutes to allow the burgers to firm up.

3. Spray a large **non**-stick frying pan with oil and set the pan over a medium **heat**. Working in batches (you need to leave enough room **between** the burgers to be able to flip them over), add **the burgers** to the pan and cook for 6 minutes on each side. **Keep warm** while you cook the rest.

4. Serve at **once with** the creosa sauce spooned over.

> **TIP:**
>
> If you want to make these burgers ahead of time, cook them, let them cool completely and store for a few days in an airtight container in the fridge. Gently reheat in a frying pan when needed.

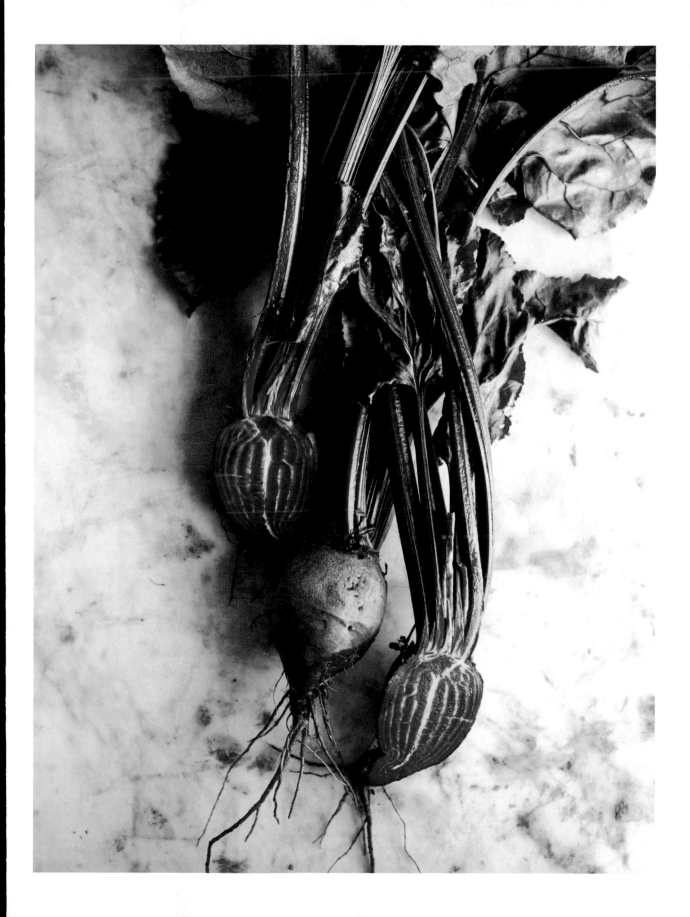

GREEN LENTIL and VEGETABLE RAGÙ

This is a different kind of Bolognese that crams in three of your five-a-day. I often make it in my diet cooking demonstrations. The husbands who have been abandoned for the day are presented with it for dinner and they all love it. This ragù is also good served with tagliatelle instead of spiralized courgettes and it forms the basis of the aubergine and lentil lasagne on page 162.

SERVES 6

olive oil cooking spray

1 onion, finely chopped

2 carrots, diced

2 celery sticks, finely chopped

4 garlic cloves, crushed

1 tbsp tomato purée

1 tbsp balsamic vinegar

250g diced vegetables, such as courgettes, peppers and/or mushrooms

1 x 400g tin of green lentils, drained and rinsed

1 x 400g tin of chopped tomatoes

1 tsp dried basil

1 tsp dried oregano

salt and freshly ground black pepper

250g courgette

2 tbsp shaved Parmesan cheese

1. Heat a few spritzes of the oil in a large non-stick saucepan over a medium heat. Add the onion, carrots and celery along with 2–3 tablespoons of water (or stock if you have some extra to hand) and cook gently, stirring often, until the vegetables are soft.

2. Add the garlic, tomato purée and balsamic vinegar and raise the heat to high. Cook for 1 minute more, then add the diced vegetables, lentils, tomatoes, basil and oregano. Bring back to a simmer, then cook for about 20 minutes. Season the ragù to taste with some salt and pepper.

3. Meanwhile, spiralize the unpeeled courgettes and divide them between six shallow bowls.

4. Ladle the ragù over the spiralized courgettes and scatter over the shaved Parmesan. Serve with a green salad and dressing (page 97) on the side.

> **TIP:**
>
> You can easily make this meaty! When you add the garlic, tomato purée and balsamic vinegar, stir in 250g turkey mince instead of the tinned green lentils. Fry for 3 minutes, breaking up the mince with a wooden spoon, then add the chopped vegetables and 50g dried red lentils. Continue as above.
>
> If you don't have a spiralizer, you can buy packs of spiralized courgettes and other vegetables in most supermarkets.

AUBERGINE and LENTIL LASAGNE

This ticks all the boxes: it's low-carb, high-fibre and hearty. You won't miss the meat.
MAKES 4

*800g aubergines (about 3),
sliced into rounds*

olive oil cooking spray

*salt and freshly ground
black pepper*

*1 batch of green lentil and
vegetable ragù (page 161)*

For the cheese sauce:

300g ricotta cheese

*100g Parmesan cheese,
finely grated, plus extra
for sprinkling on top*

2 eggs, lightly beaten

2 tsp arrowroot powder

2 tbsp water

To serve:

green salad

1. Preheat the oven to 190°C.

2. Spread out the aubergines in a roasting tin (or two) and spray each slice with one spritz of the oil. Turn the pieces over, spray again, then season with salt and pepper. Roast for 15 minutes, until they are light golden and getting soft.

3. For the cheese sauce, put the ricotta, Parmesan, eggs and a pinch of salt and pepper in a medium-sized bowl and mix together. Mix the arrowroot powder with the water in a small bowl, then add this to the cheese mixture and stir to combine.

4. To assemble the lasagne, reduce the oven temperature to 180°C. Spread half of the ragù over the base of a large lasagne dish. Using half of the aubergines, add a layer of slightly overlapping rounds, then spread half the cheese sauce over them. Repeat the layers, finishing with the cheese sauce. Sprinkle with extra grated Parmesan.

5. Bake for 25 minutes, until a knife cuts easily through the layers. Remove from the oven and leave to stand for 10 minutes before cutting into portions. Serve with a green salad.

> **TIP:**
> To replace the cheese sauce with a low-fat (and vegan) sauce, blend a tin of butter beans (drained and rinsed) with 1 tablespoon of olive oil, 1 teaspoon of lemon juice and some freshly ground black pepper in a food processor. Slowly drizzle in 60-120ml of water until you have a smooth sauce.

SAUCES

I am a totally self-taught cook. I have been cooking since I was twelve and have always loved the creativity of cooking. It was my stress-buster after a mad day at work, and the children were always delighted to do a big bake-up on a wet weekend afternoon.

The year we opened Reveries we took a two-week holiday in England, eating at fine restaurants and making copious notes of menu ideas for Reveries.

We did a sauce course with Sonia Stevenson in The Horn of Plenty in Devon, a Michelin-starred restaurant in an old country house. She is a brilliant chef and taught me the basics of sauce making, which stand to me today.

I think sauces elevate the simplest dish to a new level of flavour. They can be fat-free and starch-free but still taste wonderful.

Make your sauces in batches and freeze for later use. They will retain their flavour for up to three months.

TOMATO SAUCE

I've been making this sauce ever since we had our restaurant, Reveries in Rosses Point, Sligo, in the 1980s. I would buy overripe tomatoes for maximum flavour, and if I had time I would roast the halved tomatoes in a hot oven for 30 minutes to intensify their flavour even more. This is great for a quick meal with pasta and Parmesan or served with a chicken fillet, white fish or pork.

MAKES 500ML

olive oil cooking spray

1 onion, finely chopped

1–2 garlic cloves, chopped

6 large ripe tomatoes, chopped

300ml vegetable stock

2 tsp basil pesto

salt and freshly ground black pepper

1. Heat a few spritzes of the oil in a large heavy-based saucepan over a medium-low heat. Add the onion and garlic, cover the pan with a lid and sweat for 10 minutes, until softened but not coloured. Add the tomatoes and stock and cook for 20–30 minutes, stirring occasionally, until the tomatoes have broken down into a thick sauce.

2. Stir in the pesto, then pass the sauce through a fine-mesh sieve to remove the tomato skins and seeds (you can skip sieving the sauce if you want a more rustic sauce). Season to taste with salt and pepper.

3. You can either use this straight away or refrigerate it for up to four days in a covered container. It also freezes well in small batches for up to three months.

> **TIP:**
>
> A tin of good-quality whole plum tomatoes can be substituted for the fresh tomatoes.
>
> To enrich the sauce, try adding a couple of tablespoons of crème fraîche mixed with 1/2 teaspoon of arrowroot powder and a little water (this keeps the sauce from splitting).

LOW-FAT MILD CURRY SAUCE

As a medical student in Galway, I shared a house with my friend Helen. About once a month she would develop a longing for a curry. We would battle over the amount of curry powder. Then Helen's sister Imelda, who had neighbours who had lived in India, gave us her recipe for a curry sauce. That recipe became my standard that has evolved over the past 40 years. Recently I have learned more about curries from my friends Ahmed and Jahanara from Bangladesh. My low tolerance to chilli amuses them, but I substitute other spices. I love all the layers of flavour in this sauce.

MAKES 500ML

olive oil cooking spray

1 large onion, finely chopped

2 sticks of celery, chopped

1 garlic clove, crushed

1 heaped tbsp curry powder (or according to your taste)

1 heaped tbsp garam masala

2 tsp ground turmeric

1 tsp ground ginger

725ml hot vegetable stock

1 medium dessert or Bramley apple, cored and chopped (no need to peel)

2 tbsp grated creamed coconut

1 tbsp tomato purée or a good squirt of tomato ketchup

1 heaped tbsp mango chutney, plus extra to serve

1. Heat a few spritzes of oil in a large non-stick frying pan over a low heat. Add the onion and celery and cook, stirring occasionally, for 4 minutes, until softened. If the onions are browning too much, add a splash of water and cover the pan with a lid. Add the garlic and cook for 1 minute.

2. Stir in the spices and cook gently for 5 minutes, stirring a few times with a wooden spoon. Gradually stir in the stock. When the sauce begins to bubble, add the apple, grated creamed coconut, tomato purée or ketchup, mango chutney and some salt and pepper. Turn the heat down to simmer gently for at least 15 minutes. If adding veg, add with 100ml water and cook until it is tender.

3. Transfer to a clean jar and store in the fridge for up to a week or freeze for up to three months.

TIP:

Use any vegetables you like to make this a vegetarian curry Add the chopped veg directly to the sauce, starting with those that take the longest to cook. Cook for 10-15 minutes, covered, until the vegetables are cooked through Once the veg are cooked, simmer, uncovered, until the sauce thickens.

For a meaty curry, add 600g of raw or cooked chicken, lamb or beef, chopped into bite-sized chunks, directly to the sauce. Stir well, put on a lid and simmer gently until raw meat is completely cooked or cooked meat is heated through.

CREOSA SAUCE

This sauce is very versatile and is great with a barbecue, as it goes well with grilled fish and meat. I like to serve it with the buttermilk-marinated hake on page 145 or grilled mackerel and it's also good with the beet burgers on page 158.

SERVES 8–10

450g ripe tomatoes
(the riper, the better!),
deseeded and finely diced

225g cucumber, deseeded
and finely diced

1 red onion, finely diced

1 sweet red pepper, deseeded
and finely diced

95g gherkins, finely diced

95g capers, diced

4 tsp chopped fresh
flat-leaf parsley

1 tsp chopped fresh
tarragon

200ml olive oil

3 tbsp red wine vinegar

2–4 tbsp Dijon mustard

salt and freshly ground
black pepper

1. Put the tomatoes, cucumber, onion, red pepper, gherkins, capers and herbs in a bowl and mix together.

2. Put the oil, vinegar and 2 tablespoons of mustard in a jug and whisk to combine, then taste and add more mustard if you want it punchier. Pour over the vegetables and mix together thoroughly. Season to taste with salt and pepper.

3. Cover the bowl with cling film and leave in the fridge for a few hours or up to 24 hours before using to allow the flavours to develop. Remove the sauce from the fridge about 30 minutes before serving to allow it to come back to room temperature.

> **TIP:**
> This sauce keeps for up to three days in an airtight container in the fridge.

SNACKS

Healthy snacks are an important part of a diet plan. There will inevitably be times when you need a little nibble of something to keep you going between meals, so be sure you have healthy options to reach for instead of a packet of biscuits or crisps.

Try to have a carbohydrate and a protein at each snack. This will slow down the digestion of your food as the stomach works on both, making you feel full for longer, and it will help to keep your blood sugar levels balanced. Try a piece of fruit with a small handful of walnuts, almonds or a teaspoon of nut butter (page 187); wholegrain or wholewheat crackers or crispbreads with hummus (page 188) or pistachio and feta dip (page 192); top a crispbread with meat, smoked fish, salads or some tomato and lettuce, then sprinkle with toasted seeds and add a drizzle of dressing; or use baby gem lettuce leaves as a wrap and fill with cold leftover beef bulgogi (page 129), shredded cooked chicken, chopped egg or smoked salmon, pickles and a teaspoon of mayonnaise.

I've included a good selection of snacks here, but if all else fails, keep some 'squirrel snacks' – small bags of nuts, seeds and dried fruit that you've mixed together yourself – in your office desk drawer or handbag (but please, don't add chocolate chips!).

CRUNCHY CAULIFLOWER POPCORN

My assistant, Maria, and I were looking for snack dishes and adapted this recipe to be made with less fat. The smaller the cauliflower pieces, the better.

SERVES 6

3 crispbreads (approx. 75g)

50g walnuts

2 egg whites

2 tbsp water

1 tsp Dijon mustard

1 small head of cauliflower, broken into 2.5cm florets

olive oil cooking spray

1. Preheat the oven to 230°C. Thoroughly coat a wire rack with the oil and set on a foil-lined baking tray.

2. Put the crispbreads and walnuts in a food processor and pulse until they form fine crumbs. Tip out into a wide, shallow bowl.

3. Put the egg whites, water and mustard in a second shallow bowl and whisk to combine.

4. Working in batches, toss the cauliflower florets in the egg white mixture, shaking off any excess, then dredge in the crumb mixture, again shaking off any excess. Put the cauliflower on the greased wire rack.

5. Bake in the oven for 20–25 minutes, until the cauliflower is tender, crunchy and golden.

> **TIP:**
>
> These can be served with a dipping sauce as a snack or even as a starter.
>
> Milled flaxseeds can be added to the crumb mixture for added omega-3 fatty acids.

DATE and MAPLE ENERGY BITES

These are a great on-the-go snack, but don't eat too many – dates do contain a lot of sugar, even if it's a natural kind rather than refined white sugar.

MAKES 8–10 BALLS

100g dates, stoned and chopped

50g porridge oats

2 tbsp almond butter

1 tbsp maple syrup

1 tbsp milled flaxseeds

½ tsp vanilla extract

¼ tsp ground cinnamon

1. Blend all the ingredients together in a food processor. Using your hands, mould the mixture into small balls or squares. Put on a plate in a single layer, cover with cling film and chill in the fridge for at least 30 minutes, until firm.

2. Store in an airtight container in the fridge for up to a week.

TIP:

You could use dried apricots instead of dates.

Try rolling the energy bites in ground toasted hazelnuts for extra texture.

HOMEMADE NUT BUTTER

This is easy to make at home if you have a high-powered blender or a heavy-duty food processor.
It takes a good 10–15 minutes to process, so the motor in a lighter machine won't be able to cope.
Use any nuts you like or a mix of nuts and flaxseeds or chia seeds. Try adding a little coconut oil,
maple syrup, cinnamon or even some chocolate. The sky's the limit, so feel free to experiment!

MAKES 250ML

450g nuts (see the intro)

a pinch of salt

1. Preheat the oven to 170°C.

2. Scatter the nuts in an even layer on a large baking tray. Roast in the oven for about 10 minutes, tossing them around once or twice to ensure they don't burn. Tip out onto a plate and allow to cool a little. Roasting the nuts isn't strictly necessary, but it really helps to bring out their flavour.

3. Put the nuts in a high-powered blender or heavy-duty food processor and process for at least 10 minutes, until smooth. The mix will go from coarsely chopped to fine to smooth and eventually oily. Taste and add a pinch of salt or any other flavourings you like (see the intro).

4. Use a spatula to scoop the nut butter into a clean jar. Store in the fridge for up to one month. Take the jar out of the fridge and allow it to come back to room temperature to make it easier to spread.

TIP:

Have a little nut butter with a piece of fruit as a snack to keep your blood sugar levels stable.

LIGHT HUMMUS

Hummus usually contains a lot of oil, which, even if it's 'good' olive oil, is not ideal if you're watching the calories. My butter bean version is a tasty alternative and the sesame oil gives it an extra punch.

SERVES 6–8

¼ tsp sesame oil

1 garlic clove, crushed

1 tsp ground cumin

½ tsp ground coriander

1 x 400g tin of butter beans, drained and rinsed

2 tbsp light tahini

45ml lemon juice

salt and freshly ground black pepper

1. Heat the sesame oil in a small non-stick frying pan over a medium heat. Add the garlic, cumin and coriander and cook for 2 minutes, until fragrant. Remove the pan from the heat.

2. Put the butter beans and tahini in a food processor and blend until smooth. Add the garlic and spices from the pan and pulse to combine. With the motor running, slowly drizzle in a little water until the hummus has reached your desired consistency. Add the lemon juice to taste – you might not need all of it. Season to taste with salt and pepper.

3. This will keep in an airtight container in the fridge for up to a week.

VARIATONS:

Roast two peeled and sliced carrots with the sesame oil in a hot oven until soft. Toss with the garlic and spices and roast for a few minutes more, then allow to cool and process with the basic mix as above.

Put a raw beet on a large square of foil. Drizzle with the sesame oil, add garlic and spices and season. Wrap the foil around the beetroot and roast in a hot oven until tender. Cool, peel (use rubber gloves while peeling the beet if you don't want to stain your hands!) and roughly chop. Add to the mix and process as above. Alternatively use pre-cooked beetroot.

WHITE BEAN PURÉE

I often make this to serve with roasted red onions drizzled with olive oil and balsamic vinegar. It's also very good with whole roasted baby beets baked in foil with a little sea salt and oil, or as a dip for crudités; or try it with grilled lamb chops, chicken or roast beef.

MAKES ENOUGH FOR AN ACCOMPANIMENT TO MEAT OR VEGETABLES FOR 8 OR A SPREAD FOR 16

4 tbsp extra virgin olive oil

½ onion, roughly chopped

2 x 400g tins of cannellini beans, drained and rinsed

1 garlic clove, crushed

120ml vegetable stock or water

salt and freshly ground black pepper

squeeze of lemon juice

1. Heat 1 tablespoon of the olive oil in a saucepan over a medium heat. Add the onion, cover the pan with a lid and cook gently for 4 minutes, until softened but not coloured. Add the beans, garlic, stock or water and season with a little salt and pepper. Cook for 4 minutes, uncovered.

2. Transfer the beans and their cooking liquid to a blender or food processor with the remaining 3 tablespoons of oil and a squeeze of lemon juice. Pulse until it's the consistency you want, but I like to leave it slightly chunky. Taste and season.

3. This will keep in an airtight container in the fridge for up to a week.

TIP:

I use the vegan Marigold bouillon powder. It's widely available and low in salt too.

PISTACHIO and FETA DIP

When you're bored stiff with hummus, try this dip instead. Try it spread on the porridge bread on page 69 or serve with crispbread or crudités.

SERVES 6 AS A STARTER

100g shelled pistachios

2–4 tbsp rapeseed or olive oil

200g feta cheese

1 garlic clove, crushed

a handful of fresh dill, roughly chopped

4–5 tbsp Greek yogurt or milk kefir

1 medium lemon

salt and freshly ground black pepper

1. Put the pistachios and 2 tablespoons of the oil in a food processor and blend for 30 seconds. Add the feta, garlic, dill, yogurt or kefir and the zest of the whole lemon and the juice of one half. Pulse to combine, but don't overmix – it should have a rough texture and not be completely smooth. Add more oil if you want a smoother consistency. Taste and season with salt and pepper.

2. Serve with pitta bread, crispbreads or crudités for a lovely starter. Store any leftovers in an airtight container in the fridge for up to four days.

> **TIP:**
> You can buy milk kefir in supermarkets or health food shops. If you want to have a go at making your own, you can buy kefir grains online.

TREATS

You may be wondering what a chapter on treats is doing in a healthy living cookbook. If there's one thing I have learned over a lifetime of dieting, it's that depriving yourself simply does not work. I heard a quote years ago that I love – 'your body is a temple, but it's also a nightclub' – so go boogie every now and then and let yourself enjoy a well-earned treat!

But remember, treats are called that for a reason and aren't meant to be everyday foods. They should be limited to an occasional splurge and don't be impulsive about them. Rather, choose to have a nice slice of cake, ice cream or whatever you fancy. Up your standard – have really good cake or a premium ice cream and buy the best chocolate you can afford – and just have a little less. Think quality, not quantity.

I have included some really delicious recipes that I have been making for over 30 years, along with more recent recipes, like a chocolate avocado cake, so let yourself have fun cooking these and use a small spoon when you are enjoying them.

CHOCOLATE CELEBRATION CAKE

Everyone should have a good chocolate cake recipe for special occasions, diet or no diet.
SERVES 6–8

160g white chocolate

130ml cream

260g caster sugar

120g butter, at room temperature

4 large eggs

400g plain flour

1 tsp bicarbonate of soda

220ml buttermilk

For the white chocolate icing:

350g white chocolate

120ml cream

285g butter, at room temperature

500g cream cheese

1. Preheat the oven to 180°C. Line a deep 20cm cake tin, preferably a springform or loose-bottomed tin, with non-stick baking paper.

2. Put the chocolate and cream in a microwave-safe bowl. Melt in the microwave in 30-second bursts, stirring between bursts, for a total of 2½ minutes, until melted and smooth. Alternatively, put the chocolate and cream in a heatproof bowl set over a pan of simmering water, making sure the water doesn't touch the bottom of the bowl, stirring occasionally until the chocolate has melted. Leave to cool.

3. Put the sugar and butter in the bowl of a stand mixer fitted with the paddle attachment and cream together until pale and fluffy. Add the eggs one at a time, but don't worry if the mixture looks curdled. With the mixer running on low, slowly pour in the melted chocolate.

4. Sift the flour and bicarbonate of soda together in a separate bowl. Add one-third of the dry ingredients to the mixer and mix on low until just combined. Add half the buttermilk and mix to combine. Continue adding the dry ingredients in batches, ending with the flour mixture and making sure the batter is thoroughly combined.

5. Transfer the batter to the prepared cake tin, smoothing the top with the back of the spatula or spoon. Bake in the oven for 35–40 minutes, checking it near the end and covering the top with a piece of tin foil if it's getting too brown. Test to see if the cake is cooked by inserting a skewer into the centre. If it comes out clean, the cake is ready. Cool in the tin for 10 minutes before turning out onto a wire rack.

6. When cool, split lenghtways and fill with icing or lemon curd. Spread more icing on top and decorate as you wish.

CHOCOLATE AVOCADO CAKE

A year ago I would not have considered making a cake like this, but when I was trying out recipes for a Delicious Diet Days class, I liked the idea of a cake that tasted great but was more healthy. We had a lot of fun cooking this. One lady's eyes lit up at the thought of her two favourite foods, chocolate and avocado, in the same dish! As she is also gluten intolerant, she was delighted that it worked so well with buckwheat flour, which is gluten free. We made plums poached with sweetener and cider to accompany the cake. Needless to say, there was none left.

SERVES 2

butter-flavoured cooking spray

120g white buckwheat flour or wholewheat flour

140g xylitol or granulated sugar

100g mini chocolate chips (optional)

6 tbsp raw cacao or unsweetened cocoa powder

½ tsp bicarbonate of soda

½ tsp fine sea salt

60g yogurt of choice

60g mashed ripe avocado, measured after mashing

180ml water

2 tsp pure vanilla extract

1. Preheat the oven to 180°C. Grease a 20cm square or round baking tin or two mini loaf tins. It works best in small tins as it does not rise much.

2. Put the flour, xylitol or sugar, most of the chocolate chips (if using), cocoa powder, bicarbonate of soda and salt in a large bowl and stir well to combine.

3. Whisk together the yogurt, mashed avocado, water and vanilla in a separate bowl.

4. Pour the wet ingredients into the dry and stir until just combined (don't over-mix). Pour the batter into the greased tin and scatter over the reserved chocolate chips (if using).

5. Bake in the oven for 25–40 minutes, until the cake is well risen and a skewer inserted into the centre of the cake comes out clean. This could take as little as 25 minutes, but I find that it often takes closer to 40 minutes. Set aside on a wire rack to cool completely before running a knife around the edges of the tin and turning the cake out of the tin.

6. Put the cake in the fridge for at least 30 minutes before taking even a single bite to allow it to firm up and the flavour to develop. Trust me!

TIP:

You could double this recipe to make a double-layer cake. Try a filling of mashed avocado, yogurt and sweetener.

SIMPLE SPONGE CAKE

My mother made this cake nearly every day, either in a cake tin or as a Swiss roll. She would fill it with homemade jam, usually gooseberry, and sometimes fresh cream as well. We would have a thick slice of cake with a glass of milk as a snack when we came in from school.

SERVES 6

4 large eggs, at room temperature

120g caster sugar

115g self-raising flour, sifted

your favourite jam, to serve

softly whipped cream, to serve

1. Preheat the oven to 200°C. Line a 21cm round cake tin with non-stick baking paper.

2. Beat the eggs and sugar for a few minutes, until really thick, creamy and pale. The beaters should leave a track in the mixture. Using a spatula, fold in the flour in three or four batches.

3. Pour the batter into the lined tin and bake in the oven for 12–14 minutes. The cake will be golden brown and springy to touch and crinkled at the edges.

4. Allow to cool slightly, then loosen the edges away from the tin. Tip the cake out onto a wire cooling rack, removing the paper.

5. To serve, spread the top with your favourite jam and serve with a dollop of whipped cream on the side.

TIP:

You can substitute 25g of cocoa powder for 25g of the flour to make a chocolate version or add 1 tablespoon of instant coffee for a coffee version.

PEAR and PARSNIP LOAF CAKE

My assistant Maria and I were throwing around ideas for a cake one day. I said why not try parsnips instead of carrots in a cake and this is what we came up with! She brought it home to her men to sample and they gave it a major thumbs up.

MAKES 1 LOAF CAKE

75g caster sugar

2 eggs

½ tsp vanilla extract

75ml coconut oil, at room temperature

100g plain flour

50g wholemeal flour

1 tsp baking powder

1 tsp ground cinnamon

½ tsp bicarbonate of soda

½ tsp mixed spice

a pinch of salt

200g parsnip, peeled and grated

100g pear, peeled, cored and finely chopped

25g porridge oats

25g sunflower seeds or finely chopped walnuts

25g sultanas

1½ tbsp desiccated coconut

1. Preheat the oven to 200°C. Line a 2lb loaf tin with a paper liner.

2. Put the sugar, eggs and vanilla in a large mixing bowl and whisk for 3–4 minutes, until the mixture is thick, pale and has reached the ribbon stage or a sabayon consistency – in other words, you want to be able to make a figure 8 in the mixture with a spoon. This makes for a lighter cake. Whisk in the coconut oil.

3. Put the flours, baking powder, cinnamon, bicarbonate of soda, mixed spice and salt in a separate bowl and mix to combine, then gently fold these dry ingredients into the egg mixture, trying to keep as much air in the batter as possible.

4. Fold in the parsnip, pear, oats, sunflower seeds or walnuts, sultanas and desiccated coconut until just combined. Transfer to the lined loaf tin.

5. Bake in the oven for 10 minutes, then lower the heat to 180°C and bake for another 50 minutes, until a skewer inserted into the centre comes out clean. Allow to cool in the tin on a wire rack, then turn out and peel off the paper liner. Cut into thick slices and serve with a cup of tea.

GERMAN PLUM CAKE

The sugar draws out the plum juices, which run into the pastry and rise up between the plums so that they become embedded in the cake. Delicious!

SERVES 8

125g caster sugar

175g self-raising flour

75g cold unsalted butter, diced

1 small egg, lightly beaten

1 tbsp cognac

750g ripe plums, stoned and halved

icing sugar, to dust

1. Preheat the oven to 190°C.

2. Mix half of the sugar with the flour in a large bowl. Rub in the cold butter using your fingertips until the mixture resembles breadcrumbs. Add the beaten egg and the cognac and briefly work the mixture with your hands until it just comes together. You may need to add a little more flour if the mix is too sticky.

3. Pinch off lumps of the pastry and press into the base of a 25cm loose-bottomed tart tin. Arrange the fruit on top of the pastry, cut side up and tightly packed, cut side up, then sprinkle the remaining sugar on top of the plums.

4. Bake in the oven for 20 minutes, then reduce the temperature to 160°C. Bake for up to 30 minutes more, until the pastry is golden and the plums are very soft and have released their juices.

5. Serve hot or cold, dusted with icing sugar.

TIP:

I've also made this with the same amount of rhubarb as the plums, sliced into small discs. You may need to add another 50g of sugar and I also add 1 teaspoon of ground ginger.

SPIRALIZED APPLE TART

My spiralizer is a very simple hand-cranked one, but it does the job for me. Filo pastry is usually brushed liberally with melted butter in recipes, but here I substitute a butter spray to reduce the fat content. There are usually six sheets of pastry in a pack, so make a few of these little tarts at the one time.

SERVES 2

2 sheets of shop-bought filo pastry, thawed

butter-flavoured cooking spray (see the tip)

1 tbsp ground cinnamon

2 Granny Smith apples, unpeeled, cored and spiralized

1 tbsp stevia

crème fraîche, to serve

1. Preheat the oven to 180°C. Line a baking tray with non-stick baking paper.

2. Cut each filo sheet in half widthwise, giving you four pieces. Put the first sheet on the lined tray, spritz with the cooking spray and dust with some of the cinnamon. Put the next three filo sheets on top at different angles, spraying and sprinkling each one with cinnamon, to create a star shape.

3. Put the spiralized apple into the centre and sprinkle with the stevia. Shape the 'star' into a circle by rolling up the edges, like an open-faced galette.

4. Bake in the oven for 20–25 minutes, until the filo pastry is golden brown. Check it after 10 minutes and cover with baking paper if necessary to prevent the top burning.

5. Serve with a dollop of crème fraîche.

TIP:

The Lurpak butter spray (or cooking mist, as they call it) is the best for flavour and makes the filo nice and crisp, but I also like the Groovy Food virgin coconut oil organic cooking spray both of which can be found online.

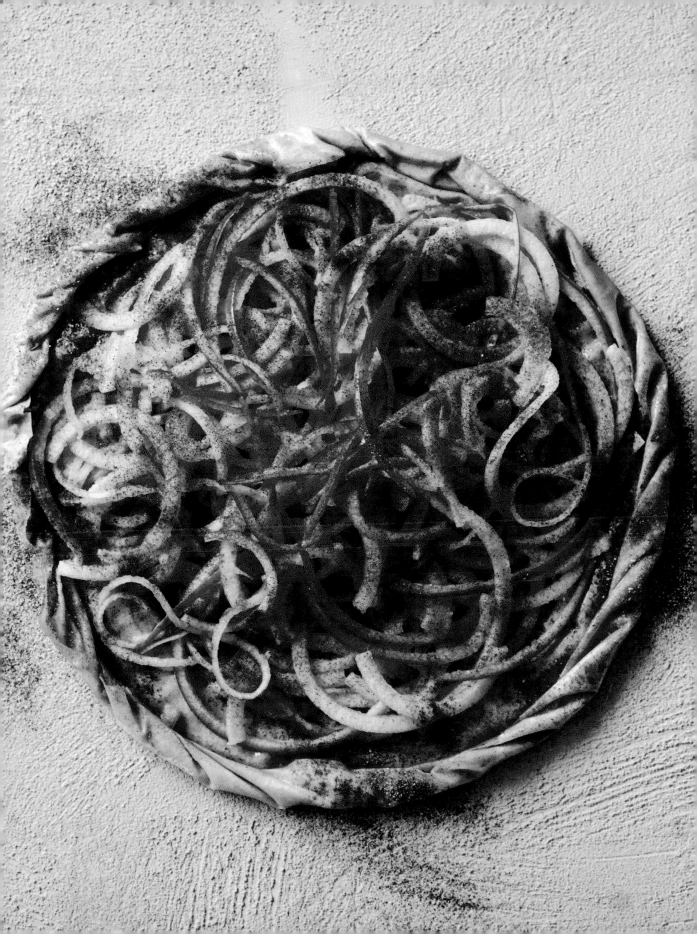

LEMON POSSET

This is one of my favourite sweet treats. The recipe was given to me by the chef in a five-star restaurant where I first tasted it. I'm asked for the recipe so often that I have copies printed off, ready for all requests! It's obviously very high in fat, so only have a small portion. It's better to have a small amount of something delish and top-quality than a low-taste, low-fat dessert that won't satisfy your sweet tooth.

SERVES 6

450ml full-fat cream

115g caster sugar

juice of 1½ lemons

lemon thins (page 210), to serve

fresh mint or sweet geranium, to serve

1. Put the cream and sugar in a large heavy-based saucepan and slowly heat until the sugar dissolves, then bring just to the boiling point. Watch it carefully so that the cream doesn't boil over.

2. Take the pan off the heat immediately and stir in the lemon juice. Pour into six containers – this is the perfect time to use those old teacups your granny gave you or even Champagne flutes.

3. Put in the fridge for a few hours, until set firm. Serve with a lemon thin on top with a sprig of mint or sweet geranium.

> **TIP:**
> You can experiment with limes or oranges as well.

RASPBERRY ICE CREAM

*This is a lovely refreshing ice cream. If you have an ice cream maker, so much the better,
but you can still get good results without one.*

SERVES 2–4

200g frozen raspberries

1 tbsp stevia

150ml sour cream

1 egg white

1. Put the raspberries and stevia in a small saucepan over
    a medium heat. Cook for 10 minutes, until the raspberries
    have thawed and broken down. Remove the pan from the
    heat and allow to cool. If you want a completely smooth
    ice cream, sieve the raspberries at this point to remove
    the seeds.

2. Whip the sour cream in a large bowl, then fold in the cooled
    raspberry purée.

3. Whisk the egg white, then fold it into the raspberry mixture.

4. Put in a shallow container and leave in the fridge to chill
    and set, then transfer to the freezer for 1 hour. Remove from
    the freezer and mix well. Repeat after another hour. Finally,
    put the container in a ziplock bag, removing all the air
    before you seal it. This stops the ice cream getting too hard.

5. Put the container in the fridge half an hour before serving to
    make it easier to scoop into small bowls.

FROZEN YOGURT with APPLE SAUCE

This creamy, tangy frozen yogurt is delicious with a slice of the spiralized apple tart on page 206 or on top of an apple crumble. Best of all, you don't need an ice cream maker to make it.

SERVES 6

300ml apple sauce (page 173)

50g icing sugar

½ tsp grated nutmeg

½ tsp ground cinnamon

zest and juice of 1 orange

300ml thick plain yogurt, whipped

1. Put the apple sauce, icing sugar and spices in a large bowl and whisk until light. Fold in the orange zest and juice, then stir in the yogurt.

2. Pour the mix into individual containers (see the tip), cover with cling film and freeze until firm.

3. About 25 minutes before serving, transfer the containers to the fridge so that it will be the perfect scooping consistency.

TIP:

This is another dessert that looks great in your granny's old china teacups!

It is very good served with fresh blueberries or a mixed fruit compote (page 58) on top.

It would be a lovely accompaniment to the summer fruit terrine on page 213.